# METAGAMA

## A Journey from Lewis to the New World

JIM WILKIE

*To Norma and Archie Gillespie and their family,*
*formerly of Holm in Lewis,*
*and to my mother, Elizabeth Arkle*
*Love to Lorna, Eoghan and Jasmine*
*And in memory of Murdina Montgomery (1903–2001)*

This edition published in 2023 by
Origin, an imprint of Birlinn Limited
West Newington House
10 Newington Road
Edinburgh EH9 1QS

www.birlinn.co.uk



First published in 2001 by Birlinn Limited
Originally published in 1987 by
Mainstream Publishing Company (Edinburgh) Ltd



ISBN 978 1 83983 036 5

British Library Cataloguing-in-Publication Data
A catalogue record for this book is available from
the British Library

Printed and bound by Ashford Press Ltd, Gosport

# *Metagama* Contents

# *Preface to the Birlinn Edition*

*Metagama* was first published in 1987 and I see from notes that I began the book in 1984. What comes to mind now about that time is how the project picked up its own momentum – something which, I suppose, is the real reward of any creative endeavour. It begins to assume a life of its own and, unlike a work of fiction, social history can breathe actual life as the characters whose story is being told begin to present themselves.

Anyone who has ever tackled Highland history is aware of the mountain of work done by predecessors and, when one reviewer eventually described the book as a 'useful footnote to the history of the Highland Clearances', I was quietly proud for, although the work managed to bring together the testimony of only a dozen emigrants, I know that such personal recollection is absolutely invaluable if the period, place and its people are to be properly understood both by myself and succeeding generations.

I am also reminded of the help I received. Out of the blue, a 20-page letter would arrive from someone who had heard what I was doing and, once personal contact had been established, another chain of communication was revealed to me. The Gaelic Resistance, it would seem, was alive and well although, 15 years later, the language remains in jeopardy.

It was immediately obvious to me that very few *Metagama* emigrants were still alive, and the fragility of their number was brought home to me when one man, James Ross MacLeod of Wisconsin, whose sister had originally contacted me from Aird Tong, died in correspondence. Today, I am uncertain whether anyone who made that historic journey remains alive.

By the summer of 1986, I was ready to cross the herring-pond but, in spite of a fairly massive correspondence, my list of interviewees was still rather depleted. One man (San Francisco) and one woman (Winnepeg) lived slightly too far away. Another man was unwell; and so it went. I had been pointed in the direction of a Lewis-born travel agent, however (Murdo MacLeod), and he made a few, valuable last-minute contacts.

My plan was to follow in the footsteps of the emigrants in order that I might guess at some of their early impressions, and from Halifax (where I was welcomed by Portree architect David Forsyth – now, sadly, also deceased) I began the long train journey through the Maritime Provinces. When the *Metagama* arrived, the St Lawrence river was icebound, so the ship had diverted to St John, New Brunswick, from where its human cargo continued their journey by train. St John in 1923 boasted the largest deep-water berthage in the world, and although in 1986 the town centre was newly-modernised, some parts of the city – like bits of Glasgow and Liverpool – retained the feel of an old-time Atlantic port with stone-built shipping offices, gable-end advertisements for 'Shamrock Plug Tobacco' and the like. Amazingly, an old cinema in which the *Leodhasachs* were given a reception was still standing and I received a splendid insight into the life of the province from my next contact – Lloyd Leland —whose wife Cathy came originally from Point in Lewis. Lloyd had grown up on a New Brunswick farm not dissimilar to a Lewis croft and, although only six years old when the *Metagama* arrived, could recall the floods which delayed the emigrants' passage and the fact that 1923 was remembered locally as 'the year of the freshet' or Spring flood.

En route to Montreal, the train passed through some fascinating territory: dense woodland of the sort that covers large parts of the Maritimes, and Quebec townships of Scotch County like Sherbrooke and Megantic, which had featured prominently in earlier Lewis emigrations. The approach to the city from the east is through a vast, fertile plain and in the suburbs of Montreal I located Murdo MacLean, a *Niseach* who left Lewis a few years after the *Metagama* to enjoy life as an actuary with T. B. MacAulay's Sun Life of Canada Assurance Company – a career path which many young Lewismen followed, courtesy of their Lewis/Canadian benefactor. Murdo's looks and laconic style were reminiscent of Bing Crosby and, not only did his yarns fill a marvellous afternoon, he even gave me a tune on his squeezebox!

My time in Ottowa and Toronto was largely spent in splendid libraries. At one point I found a short film of the *Metagama*'s arrival at St John wrongly catalogued, and this was later shown in Scotland by BBC Gaelic Television. After a week, I was headhunting again, this time over the border in Detroit. My professional background in popular music meant a visit to Motown filled me with great anticipation, but my first impression was not altogether favourable as people were generally unwilling to talk to me when I asked for directions, apart from one fellow who said he couldn't help me unless I wanted to buy some drugs!

A taxi, however, took me to the suburban home of Donald 'Tulag' MacLeod and his wife Annie and, besides his own invaluable memories, he was able to give me some information on more survivors. New York was next and I passed a major league game of baseball at the legendary Shea Stadium on my way to see Norman 'Broxy' Mackenzie. Norman – yet another *Niseach*, and with the silver hair and good looks of a Hollywood veteran – had actually sailed on the SS *Canada* in 1924, but his experiences were broadly similar to those of the *Metagama* immigrants, although he appeared to have had a particularly trying time at the hands of the US immigration authorities. He, in turn, passed me on to another splendid character, Angus MacDonald of Buffalo, whose friend, Mrs Ann Bernecky, was the daughter of Charles MacIver, founder of the Lewis Pipe Band.

Back in Toronto I had an unexpected bonus in my final days. Mr and Mrs John MacDonald of the Toronto Gaelic Society put me in touch with Mrs Mary MacIver, whose brother and husband had both sailed on the *Metagama* and whose Canadian wedding in the 1920s had been attended by her cousin Murdo MacFarlane, the Melbost bard.

I returned to Scotland with the firm conviction that a more complete story of the *Metagama* and her Lewis emigrants could now be told.

Jim Wilkie
April 2001

# *Preface*

This book is in three parts. The first is a resumé of emigration in Lewis history and its relationship to the land question. It is intended to give some background information to the reader who is perhaps less familiar with some of the complexities thereof, and derives almost exclusively from secondary sources. The earlier scholarship of W. C. MacKenzie, J. P. Day, Arthur Geddes, A. MacKerral, J. M. Bumstead, Brian Inglis, Eric Richards, Nigel Nicholson, T. C. Smout and, in particular, James Hunter, is gladly acknowledged – as is that of Lewis writers Donald MacDonald, James Shaw Grant, Frank Thompson and lain Crichton Smith.

The second part chronicles events immediately before, during and after the *Metagama* emigration, using primary sources where possible.

The third is a series of interviews which, hopefully, allows some of the surviving emigrants and others a chance to speak for themselves.

The book would not have been possible without the assistance of the interviewees and I thank them all for their kindness and hospitality. I would like to thank Christina Smith and her colleagues at Comunn Eachdraidh Nis for their help, and permission to reproduce some of their excellent work.

On a personal basis, each of the following played his or her part, and I thank them all: Murdina Montgomery, Newmarket; Bell Smith and the boys, Stornoway; Kenny 'Fags' MacDonald; Alex Morrison (Stornoway Library); Richard Langhorn (Stornoway Museum); Flora McNeill; Daisy Reid; Joyce and Jane Waters; David Forsyth; Peter MacLeod; John MacDonald (Toronto); Murdo MacLeod (Travel); Larry Spears; Michelle Myers; Norman MacKenzie (Keose); Ann and Joe Bernecky; Norman Malcolm MacDonald; Iain MacLeod; Sam Maynard; Iain MacLean; Jimmy Truearn; Marion MacLean; Sylvie Robotaille; Mr and Mrs Aimsir Eachainn; and Donald J. Macleod.

I used the resources of the Mitchell Library, Glasgow; Edinburgh University Library; Stirling University Library; the National Library of Scotland; School of Scottish Studies, Edinburgh; Department of Canadian Studies, Edinburgh University; Dundee City Library; The National Archive of Canada; the Robarts Library, Toronto; The Archive of Ontario,. Toronto; the Central Library of New York; Stornoway Harbour Commission; Stornoway Library; An Lanntair, Stornoway; St John Library; CPR archives; George Munk; Glenbow Institute, Alberta; Chingacousy Library, Ontario; Peel Archives, Brampton, Ontario; Ojibway and Cree Cultural Centre, Ontario; Scottish Record Office, Edinburgh; and I take this opportunity to thank the staff of these institutions. I am further indebted to Archie Gillsepie for reading the text and making some valuable suggestions.

Research grant assistance was received from the Scottish Arts Council and the Sun Life Assurance Company of Canada (UK Office), and loan assistance from the Highland Fund.

# Introduction

The ceilidh is central to the Highland way of life and to that of the crofting communities in particular, but no one need look out their dancing shoes or dress up for the occasion because, in its purest form, a ceilidh is simply a visit to a friend's home, a blether, a cup of tea, maybe a dram and – if the visitor is inquisitive enough – a story from the past.

One day in 1983 I was visiting the home of my wife's grandmother in Newmarket, a township on the outskirts of Stornoway in the Isle of Lewis. Murdina Montgomery was not a terribly old woman. In her late seventies, perhaps, but still strong, with all her faculties, and that dignified air of which many of the old Gaels are possessed.

I, as the prospective grandson-in-law, had been taken out to the house to meet her and her husband, Roddy. There was first the obligatory courtesy, a kiss and a cup of tea and, when Roddy excused himself for bed (he had not been very well and, sadly, was to die the following year), the rest of us – two cousins, an aunt and the cailleach herself – settled down for a ceilidh.

Murdina's speech was slightly slowed by the years but it was measured and I noticed that she pronounced the definite article as 'thee' in conversation, a habit fairly common amongst a people whose first language is Gaelic. Had she lived in this house all her life, I enquired? No, but most of her married life, and Roddy built it himself when their first child was due. And had they travelled abroad? Murdina had, to New York as a domestic servant, but Roddy had not, although his brother and sister once emigrated to Canada.

'They went on thee *Metagama*,' she volunteered.

'Thee *Metagama*.' It sounded like a spaceship obviously from the past, yet futuristic – and I pressed her further.

'It was thee emigrant ship,' she continued, diverting her eyes and wiping a hand of experience on the corner of her Rayburn stove. 'It sailed from Stornoway in 1923.'

Of course. Not *an* emigrant ship, although the people of Lewis and emigration were old adversaries even then, and two more liners would anchor in the Minch for that same purpose before the decade was out. Not *an* emigrant ship. *The* emigrant ship.

It was later that I decided to find out more about the *Metagama* and its human cargo. I was researching my first book (whose subject matter was football) in the Dundee City Library and one of my sources was the *People's Journal* of the 1920s, at that time still a fairly liberal weekly in the image of its most famous publisher, John Leng. In 1923 it carried two stories simultaneously, one concerning the difficulties faced by a Dundee football club, whose Irish ancestry was proving something of a millstone around its neck in the wake of the Ulster Treaty, and the other describing a recurrence of the perennial land question in the Isle of Lewis and one of its historical solutions – emigration.

To my astonishment but great satisfaction, I came upon two photographs. One was of the football team, Dundee Hibs, who were considering changing their name to Dundee United, and the other of a man named Murdo Montgomery, a piper journeying from Lewis to the New World, on the emigrant ship SS *Metagama*.

* * *

'There is much to be said of the Hebrides,' wrote Hugh MacDiarmid in 1939. 'They have such a complicated and romantic history; they figure in such a wonderful literature; their problems today are so intricate and controversial.

'Another consideration', he continued, 'is the fact that so much has been written about them already and is so readily available (and, indeed, so widely read) that I do not wish to re-traverse familiar ground.'

The Scottish Gael has not always received such respect from his Lowland counterpart, but the sympathetic Lowlander is often compelled to look north and west, if only to contrast the situation there with his own condition or experience. It is as though there is meaning for him in these islands – not in some mystical sense but in the knowledge that these people, his erstwhile kith and kin, have somehow managed against considerable odds to retain their land, their culture, and thereby a say in their own destiny. And this, paradoxically it would seem, in communities in which loyalty to monarchs, clan chiefs and the Church has traditionally played a prominent part.

# *Introduction*

The Island of Lewis can take us as far back in time as we wish to go. Founded on gneiss – the oldest and toughest type of rock on the face of the earth – its peat moors, rivers and lochs have provided a natural theatre of human drama since pre-history, and the Gael can trace his present-day existence with a degree of continuity to ancient forms of communal life. As often as not, however, the Lewisman in particular, as an apparently natural sailor and adventurer, has looked to further horizons and made his mark in foreign parts, in so-called theatres of war, trade or exploration, and for this reason has historically been seen as 'well-suited' to emigration.

Emigration has meant different things to people at different times, but whether voluntary or compulsory, it comes from the very heart of their being, marking those times when they themselves or their ancestors, for reasons which they did not understand or understood only too well, were required to leave their homelands in the face of changing circumstances.

A number of historical works have shown that the people of the Highlands and Islands have engaged in a protracted and spirited struggle over centuries with some of the forces of change, but there is still controversy at every level – personal, academic, governmental and so forth – regarding the interpretation of that struggle.

# *PART I*

# *EARLY EMIGRATION*

# *Chapter 1*

There was never a time when the Gael was a stranger to emigration. The hired Highland mercenary was a feature of military life in Western Europe throughout the Middle Ages, and William Shakespeare, in *MacBeth*, correctly identified the West Highlands as the place of origin of the 'Gallowglasses' *(Gallòglaich)* – Hebridean fighting men who were brought to Ireland as early as the thirteenth century to counter the Anglo-Norman invasion. Many of these men and their descendants then settled in Ireland as professional soldiers and it was not until the final English conquest of that country, in 1602, that such families lost their estates.

The subsequent colonisation of Ireland was the work of Lowland Scots, and when many of these (Ulster) emigrants again became colonists, this time as the Scots–Irish in North America, they tended to overshadow and remain separate from the small Scots–Gaelic communities of North Carolina, say, or the 'wilderness' colonies of New York, Nova Scotia or Prince Edward Island, all of which were favoured by Lewis (and Skye) pioneers.

Many pro-Jacobite Gaels were deported as a result of the 1745 rebellion, but there was little emigration as such at this time and, in any event, the truly oppressed Highlander who could not raise the cost of his own passage seldom emigrated. Instead, the more dynamic elements tended to go, and more out of hope than coercion.

The picture began to change after the Seven Years War (1756–1763), which Britain fought with France, largely in the New World. War acted then, as it has continued to do, as a kind of watershed, but the underlying causes of this, the first great 'wave' of emigration, were to be found in the Highland system of land tenure and in general government policy, or the lack of it. In Lewis, an excess population had developed on the land prior to 1745 and it had done so as a result of a feudal system in which clan chiefs were accustomed to value their estates according to population and the number of men they could bring to arms. Whereas in the Lowlands families of farm servants were simply uprooted and moved on as agricultural improvement began to filter through, because of the general isolation of Lewis and the bonds of clan, modern farming ideas did not impress clan chiefs initially and as families increased in size their acreage was simply divided into smaller portions.

This, allied to the tradition of grazing land in common, had the effect of creating social links of some significance and also a profound attachment to the land. Agricultural methods might be primitive and the clan system at times of crop failure unable to prevent destitution, but those people belonged to that land, and that land to those people.

Such sentiment, however, was never supported by legislation and when defeat at Culloden made inevitable the break-up of the clan system and suppression of Gaelic culture, clan lands previously held in trust now became the unquestionable legal property of the chief. As he adjusted to the role of landlord his social life changed and so did his attitude to the clan lands and to the clan itself.

The demand for fighting men, however, did not abate. W. C. MacKenzie reports that between four and five hundred men left the Long Island for the war with France in North America and distinguished themselves, despite heavy losses. With the peace, many officers and men remained in the colonies, acquiring land grants where previous Gaelic beach-heads had been established, but this land was only worth anything if it could be colonised, and so recruitment began in Scotland. Some soldiers were also offered tracts of land at home but rental revaluation was now underway and, hoping that the threat would deter landlords, many refused to pay the increases. It did not have the required effect, however, so they apparently then did their level best to lure friends across the Atlantic, 'frequenting public occasions with drinks, pipes and fiddles to rouse their spirits to the expedition'.

Not that people needed much encouragement. Overcrowding; the sudden rise in rents followed by a post-war slump in the price of black cattle; a succession of bad crops and occasional epidemics (an outbreak of putrid fever in 1772 led to a rumour that the plague was raging in Stornoway) – all were factors which impelled people to listen and, with assisted passage available to the poorest people in the form of indentures,[1] many considered moving.

Once again, however, it was not the poorest people who, in

the main, chose to go. A contemporary article in the *Edinburgh Courant* reports that the emigrants from the Western Isles took something in the region of £10,000 with them in total, and these 'middle-class' emigrants – tacksmen[2] and others – acted neither out of fear nor obedience. Indeed, they hoped to build a quasi-feudal society for themselves in the colonies. There was, however, the distinct duress of economic and cultural dislocation as the traditional way of communal farming came under threat and, for their poorer followers or relations, the prospect of having to serve as cheap day-labour – the cheapest in Europe, in fact – if they stayed.

The islanders voted with their sea-legs.

* * *

Before the American War of Independence (1776) there was no government policy on emigration and, before 1774, no official statistics. For this reason numbers quoted are open to question, but the first major exodus from Lewis appears to have taken place in July 1773, when arrangements were made for more than 800 men, women and children to sail to America (probably North Carolina). Fearing that he might be left with a deserted countryside, the 'Little Lord' Fortrose – soon to become the Earl of Seaforth – returned 'in haste' from London. When he enquired as to their grievances the people who remained demanded their land at the old rents; a refund of increase in rental paid during the previous three years; and the instant dismissal of the factor. The factor was not dismissed but Fortrose appears to have managed to smooth over the difficulty, probably by foregoing the increases.

In 1774 two ships, the *Friendship* and the *Peace and Plenty*, sailed from Stornoway to Philadelphia and New York respectively. Some of the emigrants were from other parts of the Highlands, but of the Lewis contingent one was the young Alexander MacKenzie, a native of Stornoway who was later to make his name with the North-West Fur Company of Canada and, more remarkably, to become the first European to cross the Great Divide of the North American continent, from coast to coast, in 1793. Such romantic individual achievements, however, sometimes obscure general conditions, and around the same time as MacKenzie was leaving Stornoway, other local children were frequently kidnapped by crews as ships loaded to maximum capacity. Since there was neither judge nor magistrate on the island, parents and even factors were powerless to act, although Seaforth did petition the Home Office on this matter.

Initially the Government did nothing about emigration, as it was feared that to forcibly check it might have the opposite effect, but it did want to bring the trade under its jurisdiction, and a form of supervision was proposed with Customs Officers (some were based at Stornoway) having the power to refuse clearance in cases where the accommodation and provision for passengers were insufficient. This was also a means of reducing the profits of shipowners who would then be compelled to raise fares and so discourage potential emigrants.

The British Goverment's first policy on emigration, therefore, was one of discouragement, and legislation to that effect (supported by Highland landlords) was eventually introduced in 1803, when a 'second wave' of emigrations swept the Highlands and Islands.[3]

* * *

With the onset of the American Revolution, the British Government feared that Highlanders – their prize soldiers and versatile colonists – would be affected by 'levelling and other dangerous American principles'. In the event the Gaels fought on both sides although, having taken the oath of allegiance, most remained on the side of the king. The revolution temporarily ended emigration and when it resumed it was to British North America (Canada) that the Highlanders turned their attention. Many Gaels had moved there in the aftermath of the war and centres of Gaelic culture had developed in Prince Edward Island, the Pictou region of Nova Scotia and the Glengarry district near Montreal.

By then, however, another development was taking place in the Highlands and Islands, and against the background of another war. It was discovered that sheep imported from the Borders could withstand the rigours of a Highland winter and sheep farmers of the Southern Uplands began to offer higher rents than had previously been obtained from farms under black cattle.

In Lewis there were fewer evictions than elsewhere at first and Arthur Geddes reports that early in the days of the sheep-farming boom a Seaforth, Francis Humberston MacKenzie, was offered double rents and refused them rather than evict the people. By 1796, however, the same man was offering the entire parish of

Uig for sale as a sheep farm, and issuing wholesale summonses of removal. His successor, James Stewart MacKenzie, was to continue in this vein. He it was who, when the family fortunes were failing, instigated another highly significant replacement of cattle by sheep stock around Broad Bay. These tacks were at Coll, Gress, and Aignish.

In his complementary area of activity, the sea and shore, however, the Leosach was faring slightly better in the early part of the nineteenth century. Kelp-making boomed during the Napoleonic Wars and a number of tacksmen turned to the fishing industry, supplying capital and enterprise as curers. The state had also begun to take an active role through the British Fisheries Society and, before 1820, it appeared that 're-location' of the population in large coastal settlements might give them an alternative and better livelihood. With the abandonment of the herring fishing bounties, however, and the collapse of the kelp trade due to the reduction of import controls, this notion lost what little credibility it had and the implications were serious for laird and people alike.

The problem was that kelping was a source of revenue but it was also an obstacle to agricultural improvement in that crofts were neglected in the pursuit of short-term financial gain. With the loss of kelping revenues, therefore, the landlords were faced with a growing 'redundant' population which occupied potentially profitable land for which it could not pay an economic rent. The solution was obvious. Sheep farming would replace kelp and people would either remove to the poorer land or emigrate. The MacKenzie of Seaforth tried for both, petitioning the Government (unsuccessfully) to subsidise emigration whilst at the same time deploying 'measures' to move people from the areas best suited to sheep-farming (Uig and Lochs), to Stornoway, Balallan, Barvas, and Leurbost. Such 'measures', of course, were evictions and James Hunter has noted the 'marked imprint' which these particular evictions made upon crofting society in Lewis. Alexander Craig, Seaforth's estate manager at Brahan, was moved to comment at the time that one settlement on waste ground at Aird Tong was 'worse than anything I ever saw in Donegal where I always considered human wretchedness to have reached its very acme'.

From the 1820s onwards, therefore, Highland emigration was usually associated with clearances in favour of sheep farmers and poor Highland immigrants now became a common sight both in Lowland Scotland and North American cities. Even such drastic solutions, however, could not solve the economic problems of the Highland landlords and, within the space of around 15 years, all of the Outer Isles (with the exception of North Uist, which was sold in 1855) passed from the hands of the traditional owners to anyone who had the money to buy.

## *Notes*

1. Indenture was a system whereby people became servants for a period of years.
2. The ordinary Highlander received his land not directly from the clan chief, but from contracted middlemen or tacksmen. In this relationship, long or even written leases were unusual.
3. A prominent advocate of Highland emigration at the time of the nineteenth century was the Earl of Selkirk who, in 1808, went into partnership with Alexander MacKenzie to buy up stock in the Hudson's Bay Company, at that point teetering on the brink of financial collapse. The partnership did not last and MacKenzie was forced out just prior to a colossal business expansion by Selkirk. In return for his agreement to supply clerks and servants, the directors of the Hudson's Bay Company granted him 16,000 square miles of Northern Canada, and it is a mark of the impact which Lewismen (and Orcadians) had already made in the 'Talamh Fuar' that the first ship destined for the Bay and Red River called at Stornoway (and Kirkwall) in 1811.

   Selkirk's vision of a Highland settlement at Red River, north of Winnipeg, was not fully realised, but many Lewismen settled there and farther north, where historical links had been established with Indians and Eskimos.

# Chapter 2

> It has pleased Providence to assign to the Chinese – a people characterised by a marvellous degree of imbecility, avarice, conceit and obstinacy – the possession of a vast portion of the earth, and a population estimated as amounting to nearly a third of the whole human race.
>
> *James Matheson, 1836*

James Matheson was born in Lairg, Sutherland, in 1796. He was the son of a Scottish baronet and was educated at the High Schools of Inverness and Edinburgh, and Edinburgh University. He was obviously a quick learner for by 1818, while still in his early twenties, he was smuggling opium into China under a Danish flag of convenience. Not only that, he was preparing to lead a rebellion of merchants against the opium monopoly of the British East India Company under whose licence he officially traded, and who themselves harboured certain corporate doubts from time to time about drug dealing.

Matheson had no such reservations. Indian opium had been finding its way into China since the eighth century and despite official Chinese opposition to the trade (indeed, the Chinese understandably wished to regulate all of their trade) the sheer size of the population meant there was inevitably a considerable black market, and the revenue paid for the Chinese tea and silk which Matheson (or the East India Company) then sold to Britain in their respectable trading capacity.

One of the first to spot Matheson's 'talent' was a fellow Scot, William Jardine, a former ship's surgeon turned merchant, and in 1828 they went into partnership as Jardine, Matheson and Company, which to this day is one of the most powerful trading concerns in the Far East. Realising the value of Matheson's earlier prospecting, they decided to begin speculating in opium rather than carrying it on commission, and their willingness to exploit an innocent interpreter who was available at the time in order to gain further commercial advantage reveals much about their business morality. Dr Charles Gutzlaff had come to China as a medical missionary, and Jardine realised it would be unwise to involve him under false pretences. He therefore told him of the opium trade which was 'so absolutely necessary to give any vessel a chance of defraying her expenses', and pointed out that the more profitable the expedition, the larger the sum the company would devote to Gutzlaff's missionary work.

Gutzlaff settled for compromise, accepting the job and distributing tracts and dispensing medicine when he had the opportunity. In that respect, he was somewhat more fortunate than another employee, a captain, who delayed his ship because of an unwillingness to load opium on the Sabbath. 'We fear that very godly people are not suited to the drug trade,' wrote Matheson. 'Perhaps it would be better that the captain should resign.'

The fact that the Chinese continued to try to restrict the opium trade, however, thereby depriving Matheson of the vast fortune which he saw as rightfully his, led him to further exhortation. Using the English language newspaper of Canton to chastise his hosts – 'the most insolent, the most ungrateful, the most pusillanimous people upon Earth' – he demanded, on behalf of the British, that an emissary be dispatched to negotiate free trade with the rest of China. No mention was made of opium, of course, and the British Government acceded to the request.

By a bizarre coincidence, in view of what was to happen later in the Highlands and Islands of Scotland, the man chosen to go was a naval hero and sheep farmer, Admiral Lord Napier of Teviotdale.

Napier knew nothing of China and not only failed in his task, he was also humiliated by the mandarins, fell ill, and died in the Far East. This was the kind of opportunity Matheson had been seeking and was quick to exploit it. He had not cared for Napier personally but, realising that the home government would feel compelled to avenge the veteran of Trafalgar, he first wrote a pamphlet in which he contrived to prove that what they were asking for was no more than the chance to introduce commercial practices based on the teachings of Adam Smith and David Ricardo, and then organised a parliamentary lobby in order to get some action.

Opinion in Britain was divided. Many were unaware of the opium trade whilst others had suffered directly at its hands. The young Gladstone, for example (whose mother was born in

Stornoway), had a sister who was an opium addict, and he wanted removal of the opium ships. Also, with bribery rife among the Chinese authorities, 'free trade' was something of a misnomer.

At this point, however, an overenthusiastic Cantonese commissioner played into Matheson's hands. Lin Tse Hsu, in an attempt to impress his emperor, ordered that all opium stocks be handed over. The merchants complied, but, following a brawl which resulted in the death of a Chinese citizen, the Custom House was closed and the British port properties blockaded. At this, the British Government under Palmerston panicked. The Indian economy depended upon opium trade and, in timehonoured fashion, a British expeditionary force was sent east in 1839.

The campaign had two stages – Palmerston was unhappy with the first treaty – and the second conflict was more savage than the first. By 1841, however, the Chinese were militarily routed and, as a result of the Treaty of Nanking, the northern ports were opened to foreign trade and the southern island of Hong Kong ceded to Britain as an 'emporiurn for trade'. Its first proprietors were Jardine, Matheson and Company.

The peace, of course, was as invidious as the war. British merchants had not been solely responsible for the armed conflict, but by claiming that such a war would open up trade with China, they had perpetrated a kind of confidence trick upon the British public, for the 500 million dollars which they then proceeded to take annually from the Chinese for opium, completely used up oriental purchasing power, and general British trade actually suffered as a result.

There were other losers. The Indian peasant farmers had long been forced to grow poppy on their best land and to no advantage other than to scrape a living. The Treaty of Nanking extended this system and more than one contemporary writer noted that 'the use of rack renting and other taxes to soak up all the purchasing power of peasants was a recipe for economic stagnation, punctuated by famine'.

In 1844, and for £190,000, James Matheson purchased the Island of Lewis.

* * *

The Highlands which James Matheson found on his return were similar in many ways to those which he had left at the turn of the

Sir James Matheson (Courtesy Stornoway Harbour Commission)

century. The emigrations of the 1820s had done little to better the conditions of those who remained, and, since it was often young and fit people who emigrated at this time, leaving behind the less healthy and the aged, the situation was in some ways worse. A number of significant changes had taken place, however, in affairs of Church and State.

The State had long been responsible for the condition of the Highlands but had usually done little to rescue the people from their hopeless position. As the nineteenth century progressed there was a growing awareness of the potential of the State, and, although nothing too dramatic was actually done, an increased legislative output served to bring the debate into the public domain to a greater extent, sometimes with interesting results.

A Select Committee on Emigration, for example, reported in 1841 that

> a well-arranged system of emigration in order to relieve the present state of destitution and as preparatory to any measures calculated to prevent a return of similar distress would be of primary importance . . .

adding the proviso that

> it seems impossible to us to carry out such a system upon so extensive a scale as would be necessary, into effect, without aid assistance from the government, accompanied by such regulations as Parliament may impose, to prevent a recurrence of similar evils.

The Poor Law Commissioners, on the other hand, reporting in 1844, stated that they

> did not consider it necessary to recommend any legislative measures for promoting emigration as a remedy for the peculiar evils under which the Highland districts labour. Were the resources of the Highlands opened up, the population might be profitably employed in their own country. Emigration, even if it were practicable on an extended scale, we are convinced, would form of itself, a very inadequate remedy.

About one thing, however, the bureaucrats were agreed. Again, from the Poor Law Report:

> Were we required to point out the cause which has the principal effect in retarding, in the case of the labouring classes in the Highlands, the progress of improvement, we should, without hesitation, assign as

> to that cause, the ignorance of the common language of the United Kingdom.

The Gaelic language, however, far from preparing for its own funeral, was enjoying the best of health. The Gaelic School Society was founded in 1811 and helped many Gaels to at least read in their own language. By 1836 in the parish of Lochs, for example, half of the population aged between 12 and 24 could read Gaelic and, since the Gaelic Bible was, initially, the only book used in the schools, the Scriptures began to take on a new significance in the lives of the ordinary people.

In Lewis, the establishment of Gaelic schools was followed by a religious revival and by 1823 the Established clergy were complaining of a 'religious frenzy which . . . has become so prevalent of late', and of 'blind daring fanatics who now infest this island disseminating wild . . . unscriptural doctrines'.

A number of lay preachers had emerged from the ranks of the crofting communities to be known as 'na daoine', 'the Men', in order to distinguish them from the ordained clergy) and, to further set themselves apart, they would often affect an unusual appearance, such as long hair or flamboyant clothes. Sometimes women fainted at their open-air meetings and James Hunter's account in *The Making of the Crofting Community* conveys the excitement of the times which, in itself, would have inspired self-confidence in people and a new belief in their ability to stand up to those who did not *live* by Christian principles, as the people now understood them.

Landlords and sheep farmers, of course, when, for example, they showed little regard for their fellow men, often fell into this category, as did some ministers of the Established Church (some of whom did not have Gaelic *and* were sheep farmers), and when the issue of patronage split that Church in the Disruption of 1843, the secession became 'a tidal wave which . . . carried the population en masse'. George Davie, in *The Democratic Intellect,* has spoken of the Free Church's Intention of 're-stating the Evangel in terms of industrial society', and its ability to do likewise in terms of the land and in the Gaelic language brought spectacular results in the Highlands and Islands. In Lewis virtually the entire population left the Church of Scotland for the Free Church, and this collective action established an important precedent, both spiritual *and* material, in crofting society.

* * *

It is questionable whether James Matheson either knew or cared much about the social/religious conditions in Lewis on his arrival in 1844. Whereas, by denying the Free Church congregation, many of his contemporaries effectively isolated themselves, there is no record of any early conflict between Matheson and the Church, or people, and such interaction would in any case have been quickly swept aside by the economic catastrophe which now visited the Highlands and Islands. For many decades the potato had been the staple crop of an agrarian economy, and when it was ravaged by blight in 1846, that economy collapsed totally.

Matheson had embarked upon an improvement scheme in 1845 which, he hoped, would turn Lewis into 'another Carse of Gowrie', and this programme was intensified to deal with the crisis. But the agricultural disaster was compounded by a collapse in money incomes from ancillary sources and the result was a terrible human tragedy. By the end of 1846, three-quarters of the population, it was estimated, were without food, and the available State relief could not effectively deal with the famine.

Matheson's conduct in these years, it must be said, was relatively humane. 'A paragon among lairds' is how one historian, Eric Richards, has recently described him, and, given the behaviour of some of his contemporaries, this is probably true. Gordon of Cluny, for example, his equivalent in the Southern Isles, was responsible for some particularly brutal evictions, and was criticised both by his tenants when they later appeared before the Napier Commission and by the Quebec Immigration Authorities of the time.

John MacKay of Kilpheder saw

> A policeman chasing a man down the machar towards Askernish with a view to catch him, in order to send him on board an emigrant ship lying in Lochboisdale. I saw a man who lay down on his face and nose on a little island hiding himself from the policeman, and the policeman getting a dog to search for this running man, in order to get him on board that emigrant ship.

Another man 'was caught and tied and knocked down by a kick', despite the fact that he had 'a dead child in the house', who was buried before his wife joined him on board.

From Benbecula, Angus MacKinnon described the fate of the immigrants in Upper Canada:

> I heard that they were so poor after landing, without food or clothing, that they died by the roadside and were buried into holes where they died.

This would not have been too far from the truth. The medical superintendent at Grosse Isle quarantine station, Quebec, reported of the same emigration:

> I never, during my long experience at the station, saw a body of emigrants so destitute of clothing and bedding; many children of 9 or 10 years old had not a rag to cover them. Mrs Crisp, the wife of the master of the Admiral . . . was busily employed all the voyage in converting empty bread bags, old canvas and blankets, into coverings for them. One full-grown man passed my inspection with no other garment than a woman's petticoat.

At one stage Gordon of Cluny tried to sell Barra to the British Government for use as a convict station, but unlike some of his predecessors, could not plead poverty as a justification. When he died he was one of the richest commoners in the country, with a fortune of between one and two million pounds.

By that time (1851) James Matheson had himself been created a baronet for his 'energy and public spirit'. This had entailed providing sustenance during the famine, assisting the passage of more than 2,000 emigrants to Canada,[1] and spending in excess of £300,000 in estate improvements, including drainage, roads, buildings and the provision of a steamer service. Almost half of that sum, however, was spent on his own mansions and grounds, with crofters benefiting little, and often providing labour in lieu of rent.

Matheson also built schools in parts of Lewis not previously provided for by parochial or Free Church schools, and paid for teachers, but they were not well patronised and eventually were handed over to the Edinburgh Ladies' Association. Neither were his agricultural improvements much of a success. The 60 acres drained and enclosed at Deanston in Uig, for example, were given to crofters but ultimately abandoned[2] as they were too far from the sea. He developed Stornoway Harbour but failed to give encouragement to the fishing industry, and his much-vaunted emigration schemes were by and large expedient as, under the new Poor Law, there existed the distinct possibility that lairds might have to contribute substantially to the upkeep of their poorest tenants. Matheson, of course, was under no financial pressure, but it remained his view that local resettlement and emigration were the solutions to the problem,

> as the redundancy of the population is notoriously the evil, emigration is the only effectual remedy to afford elbow room and fair scope for the success of the antecedent measures which, from over-population, have hitherto proved comparatively unavailing.

Those who stayed were left in no doubt as to the limits of their master's philanthropy. In the spring of 1851 it was announced that any crofter who owed more than two years' rent to the estate, and who rejected Matheson's offer of a free passage to Canada, would be 'served with a summons of removal at Whitsunday and deprived of his lands'. Subsequent evictions involved the wholesale clearance of several townships, some of which had been established in the wake of Seaforth's clearances in the 1820s. Evicted tenants were then moved to other existing townships, thus adding to the problems of congestion.

Sixteen thousand people are thought to have emigrated from the north-west Highlands and Islands in the 1850s,[3] but the fact that so many remained – albeit on the poorest land – is the rather more important statistic. Indeed, it might be said that crofting as we know it today really began as a last stand against the rapacious advance of capital in the Highlands and Islands and in the face of Government indifference to this greed: that the poor, rocky land on which many modern crofts are based represents the point at which landlords stopped short of literally driving the Gaels into the sea. It was on the Lewis estate that the fightback began.

*Notes*

1. Tenants received their passage to Quebec, inland railway fares, clothing and other furnishings.
2. 'Abandoned' places invariably passed into the hands of the sheep farmers. See also Note 3.

3. Geddes reports that in 1863, out of a total of 40 crofters in Barvas township, more than half emigrated 'with the landlord's assistance', and Donald MacDonald that North Galson was cleared in the same year 'at the tenants' own request'.

   An article in the *Stornoway Gazette*, however, of May 1963, throws more light on this time. Mary Paterson was cleared from Galson in May 1863 and died in Canada at the age of 102. Her grand-nephew, John Graham, heard her personal account, and relates it.

> The year of 1862 was apparently very wet and seed would not grow. The chamberlain refused to supply seed unless paid for and, in April 1863, the whole village emigrated to Canada except for five families who stayed in Brue, and three in Barvas.
>
> The villagers walked from Galson to Carloway where they joined an 'iron ship' that took them to Belfast and a sailing ship – the *Elizabeth* – then took them to Canada. The journey lasted six weeks and four days and the family then had to walk 120 miles to reach their settlement. Even before they left, it is reported, the area (Galson) was settled by people from Ardroil, Reef and Timsgarry who, presumably, had themselves been removed, and the remainder became part of the South Galson sheep farm.

# Chapter 3

These lands are mine, and you have nothing to do with them.

*Lady Matheson, to 300 Parish of Barvas crofters, in 1888*

The second half of the nineteenth century was a time of great progress for Lowland Scotland, with extensions to the railway system and shipping services; a great increase in population, trade and wealth; and a decrease in pauperism. The Highlands and Islands did not fully share in this progress, but between 1850 and 1870 sheep farming was highly profitable and crofters were slightly better off as a result of improved stock prices and better fishing. Their black houses were still insanitary; however their arable lands still deteriorating and their lives still occasionally blighted by the pernicious influence of certain factors.

Donald Munro was Matheson's factor from 1853–75 and frequently used the threat of eviction to enforce his will. As he was also inspector of the poor and procurator-fiscal, among other things, people were completely at his mercy, but his abuse of power was finally checked by a number of crofting families from Berneray, upon whom he attempted to serve eviction notices for the non-payment of rents. Three crofters were charged with 'assaulting an officer of the law in revenge for having executed his duty', but were found not guilty and, exposed by the case, Munro soon gave up office.

The Bernera verdict was a notable victory for the local population, but the situation remained delicately balanced, and when potato blight reappeared in the 1880s, followed by poor fishing and a detrimental change of system whereby daily fish auctions were introduced and hired hands paid a share instead of a wage, the result was widespread civil unrest and social upheaval.

This was because Highlanders now had greater expectations. They had, for example, begun to express an interest in the wider land reform movement. Such endeavours had brought results in Ireland and with the support of sympathetic Highland newspapers, their call for a Royal Commission of Enquiry was finally heard in 1883. The commission began taking evidence in May of that year under the chairmanship of Lord Napier, a former administrator of the Madras Province in the Indian Civil Service, and son of the peer who had played a significant part in the career of James Matheson.

Matheson himself had died in 1878 and was, surprisingly, eulogised by 'Clearances' historian Alexander MacKenzie, who reprinted a piece from another journal in his *Celtic Magazine*. Among other things, Matheson was said to have acquired his position 'by honest toil, persevering industry and honesty' and to have 'at all times used his influence to ameliorate the condition of the Chinese, and to establish various benevolent schemes in their interest'. In Lewis, the laird was apparently 'misled and imposed upon' by those in whom he placed his trust, but he wanted 'to leave the island and its people better than we found them', and this, in MacKenzie's view, he had accomplished. So pleased was Lady Matheson with this obituary, she had it reprinted for private circulation.

The crofters themselves, meanwhile, were going from strength to strength. The Highland Land Law Reform Association (later the Highland Land League), founded in 1883, had inherited the evangelistic leadership which earlier characterised 'the Men' and, having obtained the vote in 1884, the crofting communities proceeded to use it against Highland landlord/politicians by electing four of their own crofter MPs. The Crofters Act of 1886 then guaranteed security of tenure (though still under feudal superiority) and the right, on relinquishing a holding, to claim compensation from the landlord for improvements. It also entitled a tenant to leave his croft to a member of his family, and set up the Crofters' Commission (later to be known as the Land Court), which was empowered to fix rents and administer crofting legislation.

This was a highly significant development, but the 'land war' did not abate, because the need for crofting land was still considered a priority and nothing had been done for the landless cottars and squatters. The land raids continued, most notably at Park (which Lady Matheson had endeavoured to turn into a sporting deer 'forest' when the price of wool fell), Galson, Aignish and Coll.

'Lawlessness,' it was reported to the Scottish Office, was 'prevalent in almost every part of Lewis', and at one stage it was deemed necessary to send a detachment of marines to reinforce the local constabulary. The Park raiders were found not guilty of 'mobbing and rioting', but the Aignish men were not so fortunate and were sentenced to terms of nine to fifteen months' imprisonment.

The problem therefore remained, but the Napier Commission had also suggested that provision be made for assisting emigration by State advances and State direction, and, by way of diversion, the Government responded to this in 1888. Ten thousand pounds were to be made available to finance a colonisation scheme for crofters and cottars of the congested districts of the western Highlands and Islands – provided £2,000 could be raised by private subscription. The money was immediately forthcoming and 30 families were selected from Lewis and Harris to sail to Canada. They settled in Killarney, Southern Manitoba, and the following year another 49 families went out from Lewis, Harris and North Uist, to Saltcoats in the same state. The loans were found to be insufficient on both occasions, but whereas the Saltcoats settlement was a complete failure, the Killarney settlers succeeded in repaying the entire balance of the sum originally lent to them (£120).

Thus ended the first serious State experiment to remove the 'surplus' crofter population.

## *Note*

1. The crofters' language was still under pressure. The Education Act of 1872 made education compulsory, but not in the medium of Gaelic, and even the Highland Agricultural Society was, apparently, in favour of its restriction. James Mollison, an agriculturalist, wrote in the report of 1878:

> The Gaelic language may be what it likes, both as to antiquity and beauty, but it decidedly stands in the way of the civilisation of natives making use of it, and shuts them out from the paths open to their fellow countrymen who speak the English tongue. It ought, therefore, to cease being taught in all our schools. We are one people and ought to have but one language.

# *Chapter 4*

Land raiding continued intermittently until the outbreak of the First World War. The crofting economy was looking healthier as the new century dawned, with the cottage-based Harris tweed industry taking its first tentative steps on pedal looms and the herring fishing booming, but the cottars of Berneray (1901), Shawbost (1909) and Reef (1913) to name but a few, could not be pacified without land, and there was even a recurrence of religious disturbance – at Ness, in 1902 – as the Free Church fought for its continued independence.

Much of the land raiding was caused by sheer frustration, for the settlement of farms was now recognised in official circles as at least part of a solution, but Duncan Matheson – James Matheson's nephew and successor when Lady Matheson removed to the South of France – could not quite bring himself to agree.

The First World War reshuffled the cards. By the Small Landowners (Scotland) Act 1911, the Scottish Land Court had taken over from the Crofters' Commission, and the Board of Agriculture from the Congested Districts Board, but the war served to delay any resultant action and the Scottish Land Enquiry of 1917 returned to the theme of emigration, which had continued to hold its attraction, for some Lewismen in any event.

At least one senior politician, however (Lord Advocate T. B. Morrison), was quoted as saying that as soon as the war was won, the land question in the Highlands would 'be settled once and for all . . . everyone is agreed that the people of the Highlands must be placed in possession of the soil'. Well, the war was indeed won – at immense cost to Lewis[1] – and the tragedy was compounded by the sinking of the *Iolaire*, when the lives of 200 returning servicemen were lost within sight of Stornoway. At one stage during the war the Government considered buying the island with a view to pursuing a land settlement policy when Matheson advertised it for sale. The Local Government Board Report of 1916 stated:

> Lewis is always referred to as an insoluble problem. In point of fact it is no problem at all. During the last thirty or forty years, the proprietors

> of Lewis Estate have done everything in their power to thwart the economic development of the inhabitants of the island. Whatever would improve the condition of the people has been strenuously resisted because, it was argued, improvement would make people stay at home, whereas the state wanted them to emigrate . . . The Lewis native is rather wonderful in some respects. That he should have clung to his rocks and increased, in spite of such discouragement proves him to be the most virile and enduring of the Celtic stocks.
>
> The congestion of population in Lewis is incredibly bad and utterly unnecessary. In order that the centre of the island might be utterly untenanted and let as grouse moors, the people have been condemned to live on a mere fringe of land around the coast . . . The centre of the island is supposed to be common grazing for the crofters; but as a matter of fact it is so extensive and so remote from the crofts that it exceeds by four or five times what people can possibly use. Whatever land is good and capable of being ploughed is withheld from the crofters and left as separate farms. The condition of the Lews has been allowed to become so desperate that it is not possible for any individual proprietor to deal with the problem.
>
> The only solution is that the Government should buy the island and govern and regulate it as a British colony.
>
> The Lewis people are strongly of the opinion that they should not be forced to emigrate while their own island contains illimitable square miles; and after the war, unless effective steps are taken to ameliorate the situation, I am informed that violent measures will be adopted to secure land for crofters.

Subsequent events would suggest that the author of that report had his finger on the pulse, but his suggestions were ignored and Lewis (and later Harris) was purchased in 1918 by the unlikely figure of Lord Leverhulme, for £143,000.

A 70-year-old Lancastrian who was used to success, Leverhulme was a throwback to an earlier time, a Victorian entrepreneur whose manufacture and sale of mass-produced soap products had made him one of the world's leading industrialists. His drive for capital, however, was tempered by nineteenth-century liberalism and he hoped to develop Lewis with some regard for people's lives. His plans were ambitious – to introduce modern fishing and fish processing to Stornoway, to modernise and extend the harbour facilities, and reconstruct the town – and, as far as rural Lewis was concerned, besides ideas for road and even railway construction,

Children and Black Houses – rural Lewis at the turn of the century

he had distinct views on the question of the sporting aspects of his estates:

> Of course it would be impossible to develop Lewis commercially, put railways through the island, construct docks and harbours, plan herring canneries and at the same time maintain the sporting attractions of the island, but my instincts lead towards men and women and not to salmon and grouse and deer, and if the interests of the two clash, the salmon and deer must go.

Leverhulme also appears to have had some knowledge of the history and global achievements of Lewis men and women and often spoke highly of them, but such was his life's experience, he could not ultimately see his investment in anything more than economic terms and, put simply, he believed that he had to develop the fishing potential of the island at the expense of its agricultural 'system'.

The problem, of course, was that the crofters themselves did not see crofting as a job but as something central to a way of life which also involved fishing and other activities. Though they did not oppose Leverhulme's plans in principle – for any ancillary income was welcome – there was no possibility of them giving up that way of life in return for the promise of an assembly-line job

Cromwell Street, Stornoway, in the 1920s (Courtesy *Eilean nan Fhraoich* magazine)

with a town house and garden. Indeed the people of rural Lewis wished to extend the land tenure system and pressed for the land redistribution which had been promised. Leverhulme resisted this and, in particular, the break-up of the Coll and Gress farms near Stornoway which, he maintained, were needed to supply the town with milk. The Government initially went along with him to give him time to develop his scheme.

A number of cottars, however, mostly ex-servicemen, were not prepared to wait. In point of fact, between 1919 and 1923 there were incidents throughout the island at Carnish, Ardroil, Aline Deer Forest, Reed Farm, Croir, Tolsta, Galson, Garynahine, Ornsay, Stornoway, Lochs, Laxdale and Sandwick, but it was the Coll and Gress raiders – Bodaich Bhack – upon whom attention was focused. In the spring of 1919 they occupied the farms and staked out smallholdings and, in spite of considerable opposition throughout Lewis, they stuck to their beliefs and raided again after a brief withdrawal to allow the Board of Agriculture more room for manoeuvre.

In a sense it was another classic confrontation – the crofters and the millionaire landlord – but this time it was the landlord, Leverhulme, who was forced to give way. With the loss of the East European markets following the war and the Russian Revolution, the herring trade was a shadow of its former self. There were other financial problems elsewhere in his business empire. And when the Secretary of State for Scotland, Robert Munro, demonstrated some ambivalence on the question of land raiding, the great industrialist recoiled in horror. In 1921, much to the consternation of his supporters throughout Lewis, he switched his attention to Harris, and gave up on its northern neighbour.

I think it fair to say that everyone – including the raiders – had seen in Leverhulme's schemes the possibility of mutual advantage. The issues involved in the land question by then, however, were widely understood and, if Leverhulme could not resolve them, then history suggested – insisted – that he must make way for further Government action in the form of land settlement on compulsorily purchased estates, where necessary. For many young Lewis people though, the land eventually settled was not in Lewis but in North America.

*Note*

1. Lewis is said to have lost proportionately more lives in the First World War than any other community in the British Empire. From a population of 29,500, 6,700 young men joined the forces (22.7%) and 1,151 died (17 per cent of the recruits).

# *PART II*

# *THE METAGAMA EMIGRATION*

# Chapter 5

Metagama is an Algonquin Indian word which means 'where the waters meet', and the famous 'roar' of the 'twenties was surely that of a great confluence – of events, action and ideas. Certainly in Lewis the forces of historical materialism had seemed to triumph as Leverhulme departed and the people's traditional right to their land was finally confirmed.[1] Paradoxically, it was in the new home of capitalism that the ambition of the younger generation appeared to lie.

Perhaps the comradeship and education of war precipitated a collective venture to the western hemisphere. Undoubtedly, Leverhulme's failure was a constituent part of the catalyst for change. And it was a fact that emigration had been 'bottled-up' during wartime. Such things, however, do not satisfactorily explain the apparently sudden decision of around 800 young Leosachs to emigrate to Canada in a 12-month period during 1923–24.

It is clear that a general motive was the pull of opportunity elsewhere. Most Lewis families had continuing contact with the other side of the Atlantic, and these uncles who worked on the railroads and sisters who found employment in the American cities were always able to send some money home, so the more positive aspects of American emigration were never far from people's minds. Secondly, there were a number of Lewis-born soldiers in the Canadian regiments who stayed on after the war in the hope that Leverhulme might facilitate their permanent return. Accurate comparisons of opportunities were therefore readily available and one thing that was known was that the farms and developing industries of North America were intensely labour-hungry. And whilst US and Canadian trade unions opposed the introduction of skilled labour, there was no interference with labourers immigrating with a view to working in agriculture. All of this, combined with the fact that the crofting legislation now confirmed the security of elderly parents, made America an even more attractive proposition than before.

More important than such pull factors, however, was the new

push of Government policy. A number of reports were issued, some of which had been instigated by the high emigration figures of the pre-war years and, following an enquiry into the natural resources of the self-governing Dominions, an Overseas Settlement Committee was established. Its main purpose was to deal with the problems of post-war reconstruction, and the change of title from 'Emigration' to 'Overseas Settlement' reflected a subtle reappraisal of history.

It was true to say that State-aided emigration was not a new idea and, indeed, one which went back to the Napoleonic Wars. At no time, however, was this emigration ever put forward as anything other than a means of ridding the mother country of its so-called surplus population. There may have been vague notions that some would prosper in foreign lands, but the new claims of the Commissioners that 'the Empire as it exists today was largely built up by a policy of State-aided emigration inaugurated one hundred years ago . . . a policy which influenced the world's history . . .' were fanciful in the extreme, and the Canadian authorities were quick to point out that it was, in fact, the first time that the mutual benefits of emigration were acknowledged by the United Kingdom. Canada had followed an aggressive peopling policy since the late nineteenth century, and the racist nature of this policy meant that they welcomed white settlers with open arms (after British and French, the decreasing hierarchy was something like Scandinavians, Germans, Ukranians, Jews, Italians, Slavs, Greeks, Syrians and Chinese).

Initially, assistance was provided for ex-servicemen, ex-servicewomen, women generally and children, but British male unemployment showed no signs of decreasing and with the passing of the Empire Settlement Act of 1922, which made provision for assistance by grant and loan, considerations of military service and sex went by the board and emigration moved into overdrive. By the provisions of this Act, the United Kingdom would co-operate with individual Dominions on a 50–50 basis with a view to establishing a comprehensive policy of land settlement, and the Canadian authorities – the Dominion Government, the Provincial Governments and their respective agents – were quickly off the mark.

An ordinary third class fare (1922–23) was approximately £16

($80), and single men for the first time could receive an advance of up to 100% of the cost of the journey, if nominated by

(a) a British subject resident in Canada;
(b) the Dominion Government or its agencies; (c) a Provincial Government or its agents;
(d) any approved organisation in Canada provided that persons nominated are proceeding to farm work.

Single women were to be encouraged by a £6 rebate after one year's residence. This was, in effect, a bonanza for a whole range of companies, agents and other interested parties, and the steamship companies, in particular, were well prepared.

The Canadian Pacific Railway Company was incorporated in 1881 to build a railway across Canada to make the Confederation of 1867 a reality. To ensure that there was traffic going each way, the company decided to establish a steamship service, first in the Pacific, then the Atlantic. Initially it depended upon the steamships of other companies, but, this proving unsatisfactory, it first took over a number of shipping companies and then – with a view to developing a new class of traffic on the North Atlantic – it contracted with the Barclay Curle Yard on the Clyde to build two cabin-class ships, the *Missinabie* and the *Metagama*, which were the names of two of its railway stations in Northern Ontario. Emigration, of course, had always been a major factor in CPR thinking and a land agent was appointed in London even before the railway was built, to encourage people to emigrate to Canada (and travel on the railway).

The *Metagama*[2] was launched at Scotstoun, Glasgow, on 19 November 1914 with cabin class for 516 passengers and third class for 1130. It sailed from Liverpool initially and later from the Clyde, and acquired the reputation of being a 'bride ship' after the First World War, through its transporting of young brides-to-be from Scotland to North America.

## Notes

1. The situation, of course, owed nothing to ideology, although the Glasgow socialist, John Maclean, did at one point visit Lewis to warn of what he saw as the next imperialist conflict and the strategic

importance which the Hebrides would assume therein. 'Specious claptrap,' said the *Gazette*.

2. *Metagama* 7,655 tons (net); 12,420 (gross); Dim. 520ft oa; 500ft 4ins x 64ft 2ins x 37ft 10ins; Eng. Tw. Scr; quad exp; 2 x 4 cyls 26ins, 37½ins, 77ins; Stroke 51ins; 9,000 HP; 8 boilers; Stm Pr 215 lbs; 15½ knots;

   By Builder H. Steel: 3 decks; 7 holds; bridge 240ft; Coal 2,380 tons at 130 tons per day; Pass. Cabin 1,138; 2 funnels; 4 masts.

# *Chapter 6*

How you gonna keep 'em down on the farm after they've seen Paree?

*Popular post-World War I song.*
*(Donaldson/Lewis/Young)*
*Pub: B. Feldman & Co. Ltd.*
*Artiste: Eddie Cantor.*

Manning Doherty was a Canadian of Irish descent, but, as a prosperous farmer in the English outpost of Peel County, Southern Ontario, his politics were Conservative and Unionist. At that time, a Catholic could not attain the highest office in Protestant Ontario, but his political prospects took an upward turn during the First World War. Taking a lead from the United Farmers of Alberta, Doherty and his fellows founded the United Farmers of Ontario in 1914. They would have been content to remain a farming pressure group, but for the events of wartime.

Canada had entered the war with enthusiasm, and, since food was needed urgently, farmers were exhorted to produce to the limit. Farm help was scarce, however, and prices low, and only a Unionist pledge to exempt farmers' sons from conscription in order that production might be maintained prevented outright revolt. When the Government then reneged on that promise and compounded the insult by conscripting along party lines, a wave of indignation swept farming communities all across Canada.

In January 1919, the Ontario farmers (UFO) decided to take direct political action and, on a platform of abolition of political patronage; reafforestation; the establishment of a provincial highway system to cope with the growing number of cars; public development of hydro-electric power; strict enforcement of liquor laws; and an investigation of the lands and forests departments – in other words, a better deal for rural, conservative Ontario – they came to power as the majority party in a coalition with Labour.

Doherty had initially maintained his Unionist allegiances, but had been persuaded to stand for the UFO in Peel County (near Toronto) and was seen as a potential leader before losing to the

Tory. The Premier's job went to E. C. Drury, but, recognising administrative ability, Drury quickly secured a scat for Doherty in Kent County, and appointed him Minister for Agriculture. To this was then added responsibility for colonisation, in place of the local Soldier Settlement Board.

The programme of reform was quickly embarked upon. Roads were improved, a massive powerhouse begun at Niagara Falls and, as if to demonstrate that there was nothing provincial about their vision, the research programme of Banting and Best was given heavy financial support, a move which resulted in the discovery of insulin, the treatment for diabetes.

Medical research, however, was not a vote-catcher among farmers, and the local Tory press was only too happy to rumble with disillusionment and discontent. There was even a Bolshevik smear at one point, but the real problem was that the rural labour force of Canada was being attracted in ever-greater numbers to the car factories across the border and, no matter how bad unemployment was in Canadian cities, men and women could not be persuaded to work on farms. The money was just not good enough.

By 1922 there were signs that the post-war slump was ending. This meant that the demand for experienced labour on farms would become even more acute, and news that the British Government, through its newly created Overseas Settlement Committee, was prepared to spend £15 million per annum for 15 years in order to 'help relocate surplus labour' in the Overseas Dominions, could not have come to the UFO at a better time – election year.

With the smell of cheap labour wafting across the Atlantic, the London-based Agent General for Ontario, Mr W. C. Noxon, was recalled, and a summer conference scheduled in Toronto for all interested parties. It concluded:

> This conference is of the opinion that the Government of Ontario would be justified in adopting, in co-operation with the Imperial Government and Federal Government, a sane, aggressive immigration policy with the object of increasing settlement in rural Ontario and developing the natural resources of the Province; and this conference is of the opinion that in developing such policy, careful consideration should be given to the following features:
>
> The bringing-out and placing of experienced farmers with families

> by making provision for living accommodation on lines acceptable to the immigrant and the farmer;
>
> The encouragement of farmers with capital and the extension of loans now available to farmers of three years residence in the Province;
>
> The continuation of immigration of domestic servants and farm labour with such assistance for transportation and reception and supervision as may be found practical.

The actual logistics were to be handled initially by the agent general, who was to return to London and recruit 'desirable' immigrants as soon as possible. Single men, women and families were to be placed on farms in Southern Ontario for a year, and should they prove themselves the type of settler Canada wanted (and needed), the plan was then to offer them land parcels of their own farther north in what is known (rather dauntingly) as the 'Claybelt States', an area south of Sudbury which the Soldier Settlement Board had earlier failed to colonise satisfactorily.

Unfortunately, through negligence, many of the records of the Department of Agriculture and Colonisation have been lost, but nowhere at this (early) stage was there any specific mention of the Hebrides as a likely area of recruitment. On his return, the agent general instigated a thorough and wide-ranging publicity campaign which took his staff to the cinemas of Lancashire as readily as to the village halls of the Scottish Highlands and Islands.

When the *Metagama* emigration finally got under way, journalists and representatives of the Ontario Government were often at pains to emphasise that the first move had come from Lewis, However, there is no evidence to suggest that this was indeed the case. On the available evidence, the *Metagama* emigration was a Lewis response to a Canadian initiative. And the Canadians were prompted by British Government policy.

# *Chapter 7*

'. . . a lightning conductor'

The Board of Agriculture for Scotland are of the opinion that there is little real congestion in Skye, North Uist or South Uist. In Lewis and Harris, however, it is serious and to a less extent in Barra, and with the approach to exhaustion of nearly all the farmland available for distribution among the crofters, it is obvious that the natural increase of population must emigrate . . .

In Lewis the population is mainly seafaring. The late proprietor made some farmland available to the Congested Districts Board but, speaking generally, comparatively little in the way of Land Settlement has been done in Lewis. It should be pointed out, however, that the conditions in Lewis are not similar to those prevailing in other islands; the existing farms are on a smaller scale and the total area available for smallholdings is comparatively small so that the division of the present farms could in any event do little compared with what it has been possible to achieve in Skye and the Uists. Eight farms were secured and settled last spring (1921) and schemes are now in progress for four other farms, but when all the available, suitable land is converted into smallholdings there will still be left fully 500 applicants unprovided for.

The conditions under which many of the Harris and Lewis applicants live, are so uneconomic that it would be of benefit to them and also to the state if they could be induced to migrate or emigrate. Both islands are over-populated, despite a steady exodus during the last 20 years; these places can never maintain their present population in comfort, in fact, it is largely the earnings of sons and daughters away from the islands which support the homes. Fishing, weaving and every industry in the islands are at present at a standstill and the time is opportune for schemes of migration and emigration.

It was for many years difficult to induce people from these islands to migrate, but that feeling is much less strong and, given reasonable prospects and State-aided passages, it is believed that a large number would take advantage of the opportunity of bettering their position.

This Board of Agriculture for Scotland memorandum was written in January 1922, prior to the passing of the Empire Settlement Act, and, unlike the diametrically opposed Local Government

Report cited earlier, is the kind of document which would have brought some relief to a Government – the Lloyd George Coalition – which was appearing to stagger from one crisis to the next. It had blundered into Russian intervention, poisoned Ireland with the Black and Tans, and was facing desperate problems of unemployment at home. Another land war was threatening the Highlands and Islands owing to the general breach of the land settlement promise, and an escalation – given the recent Russian experience – was to be avoided at all costs. What followed was nothing short of a conspiracy which aimed to get rid of the surplus and occasionally troublesome population, without the various Government departments – the Board of Agriculture (BOA), the Scottish Office (SO), and the Overseas Settlement Committee (OSC) – losing face.

A conference was held at the London Office of the OSC with the express purpose of obtaining suitable settlers from the crofting counties of Scotland. It was estimated that there were 9,500 applicants for smallholdings – the vast majority in the Highlands and Islands – and that two-thirds of them were of a type 'suitable for settlement overseas'. The existing BOA schemes, it was thought, could absorb 1,500, and of the remainder, 1,780 were first-preference ex-servicemen. There was an obvious difficulty, however, in bringing the OSC schemes to the notice of applicants generally, in that the BOA might be charged with 'endeavouring to get rid of their responsibility'.

It was nevertheless decided to draft explanatory application forms – 'These overseas schemes are, of course, additional to, and not in place of, Scottish Land Settlement Schemes' – and to get some names and addresses from the Scottish Office.

> The question was raised whether such schemes could properly be brought to the notice of those applicants for small holdings in Scotland whose applications are unlikely to be, dealt with for some considerable time, and it was finally decided to enquire whether a list of names of such applicants could be furnished to this office. (Letter: G. Plant (OSC) to SO. 2.10.22.)[1]

The Scottish Office was rather more experienced in such delicate matters and rejected the plan, ostensibly on the grounds that it would 'mystify' applicants in the absence of general publicity for the OSC. The real thinking, however, became apparent some months later in a communication from P. J. Rose of the SO to Charles Weatherill of the BOA (7.2.23.).[1]

> It seems clearly desirable that the 'schemes' prepared by the OSC in the Dominions should be brought to the notice of possible emigrants from the Highlands and other parts of Scotland. Difficulties arise in connection with the methods. The existing raids, about which correspondence is proceeding, illustrate the difficulties.
>
> There is an obvious risk that applicants for holdings and their advocates will attack the Board with the charge that the Board are co-operating in an emigration scheme in order to cover up the deficiences of the Board's Land Settlement Schemes.

The SO preferred to exhaust alternatives and suggested advertisements, taken by the OSC or Overseas Governments, in the *Oban Times* and other Highland newspapers.

> Of course the government may be criticised whatever procedure is adopted on the general ground that emigration is an unsatisfactory substitute for land settlement. But the advertisement procedure *removes the Board from the position of being a lightning conductor.* [Author's italics.]

Weatherill wrote back immediately (10.2.23), suggesting that a letter from the OSC or Noxon to the Press Association explaining the scheme and its advantages would be just as effective and less costly, and in an interesting footnote said, 'I am having a letter [sent] to Mr Noxon. I notice that he has already been active in the Hebrides.'

He had indeed. Noxon, the eager beaver, saw no contradiction in offering Lewismen a piece of Canada in settlement of their 'land fit for heroes' wartime pledge, and wrote to the BOA (9.1.23) asking for names. That same day he was quoted in the London *Evening News*:

> A representative in the Hebrides is arranging the party. Although there is a surplus of agricultural workers in other parts of the country I could riot find the same quality (as) in the Hebrides.

The Scottish Office and the Board of Agriculture were delighted. Noxon's swift and independent action had got them off the horns of a dilemma. 'I think Mr Noxon has shown the way.' (Letter: Rose

(SO) to Weatherill (BOA) 12.2.23).

One other thing was agreed in private. Whereas it was initially thought that training for Canadian farm work might first be given in this country, the Scottish Office was later to have second thoughts: '. . . it would cost less and save a lot of trouble to send men out without any training.' (Letter: Rose (SO) to Weatherill (BOA) 8.8.22).

* * *

Mr Noxon's correspondence with Lewis has not been preserved, but the initial response to his circular can be guessed at from a Scottish Board of Health Report of June 1923. Murdo MacLean, 'Murchadh nam Bochd', was the local inspector of the poor in Stornoway, and when a scheme for emigrating whole families from Lewis was put forward in the December of 1923 (poor people were always a good target for such schemes), the Scottish Board of Health was asked to participate. 'The local inspector of the poor,' said their report, 'is of the opinion that such a scheme will largely be taken advantage of.' By that time, of course, the *Metagama* had sailed, but the quotation is none the less significant inasmuch as Murdo MacLean had more than one job. He was also the shipping agent.

Shipping agents were an early form of travel agent who, for historical reasons, usually had experience of emigration traffic. MacLean's adverts had appeared many times in the *Stornoway Gazette,* but he had never known a response like the one which greeted his eight-inch single column of Friday, 25 January 1923.

It was known locally that the Board of Agriculture had received a large number of applications for crofts, but these included many from older men with families. MacLean's new advert, for single men and women, brought a whole new dimension to the fore because the Ontario representative, a Major Goodliff, had been active for some weeks, and by the end of January his magic lantern had entertained informal gatherings at schools in Stornoway, Balallan, Leurbost, Garrabost, Ness, Barvas, Shawbost and Carloway. The deal, said Goodliff, was that if they could raise a few pounds for the fare (officially 25% of the total) and landing money, their passage to Canada would be secured by the Provincial Government of Ontario (PGO).[2] For the next year, the men would work as farmhands in Southern Ontario and from their wages –

# CANADA.

DOMESTIC SERVANTS FOR ONTARIO.

WANTED, for ONTARIO, DOMESTIC SERVANTS for FIRST-CLASS FARM HOUSES.

***TO SAIL IN APRIL.***

***SITUATIONS GUARANTEED.***

***ASSISTED PASAGES.***

In placing, the Girls in Situations every effort will be made to place them as near each other as possible.

IMMEDIATE APPLICATION should be made to MAJOR GOODLIFF, ONTARIO GOVERNMENT REPRESENTATIVE, at

**46 POINT STREET, STORNOWAY.**

# CANADA.

FARM WORKERS FOR ONTARIO

WANTED, for ONTARIO, FARM WORKERS

***TO SAIL IN APRIL.***

***WORK GUARANTEED.***

For further particulars apply to MAJOR GOODLIFF, ONTARIO GOVERNMENT REPRESENTATIVE, at

**46 POINT STREET STORNOWAY**

***Immediate Application should be made.***

*Stornoway Gazette*, 25/1/23

30 dollars a month, plus keep – they would repay the PGO as and when they could. Women would go as domestic helpers, also on farms.

Financially, the young men were not too impressed. Thirty dollars a month was only £1.50 a week and on Leverhulme's Ness to Tolsta road some had been earning £2. The road project was no longer an option, however, so the offer of a job was more than they were going to get at home. What did weigh heavily with them was the chance to see the fabled North America.

In the event, around 300 men and women[3] decided to take the plunge (although there were more enquiries initially) and Goodliff returned to London delighted – particularly with what he had seen of Hebridean 'stock'.

Given the large numbers and availability of harbour facilities, an arrangement was made with Canadian Pacific for one of its ships to make an off-line call at Stornoway and, from that point onwards, the word *Metagama* – the name of the ship chosen – was destined to find a special place in Lewis history.

That it was taking away so many fine young people was reason enough for this to be so. The psychological watershed between Old World and New, old landlordism and new – both at home and abroad, as it transpired[4] – was bound to make its mark. But there is another reason – perhaps less valid, but equally potent – why *Metagama* has become part of the Lewisman's twentieth-century world view. In a century in which the mass media would become all-pervasive, the emigration of 21 April 1923 was the island's first mass-media event.

The national press had been to Lewis before, during Leverhulme's term of occupancy, and indeed as far back as the land wars of the 1880s, but this was something completely different, both in variety and scale. This time, not only could Gaelic exiles throughout Scotland, England and North America *read* about their relatives in newspapers, they could now *hear* about them on the wireless. Even more astonishing, they could actually *see* them, courtesy of the new phenomenon of film. The Leosachs might not yet be in the main feature but there they were, as large as life, on the cinema newsreels of the Western World.

The impact must have been colossal and, for locals, compounded by the sight of an army of reporters, photographers and kinematographers disembarking at Stornoway in the spring of 1923 from the largest ship that had ever anchored in the Minch.

*Notes*

1. Files of the Department of Agriculture and Fisheries (West Register House, Edinburgh).
2. Recollections of the exact sums asked for vary, from £5 passage money to £5 landing money. Most paid nothing, however, and many entered Canada with as little as £1.
3. The shipping register of Stornoway Pier and Harbour Commission records that 315 emigrants embarked. The list of Lewis emigrants, however, numbers only 260, including 18 women. (*Stornoway Gazette* 26.4.23). The remainder came from the Uists (11), and elsewhere in the Highland area. One family, for example, is listed as coming from Gairloch.
4. In 1923, Lord Leverhulme offered the island to its people. A trust was established on behalf of the people of the parish of Stornoway to take advantage of this generous offer and, to this day, periodic elections are held to choose representatives.

   The unique aspect of this arrangement is that although the trust owns the land on behalf of the people, each crofter has retained the tenancy of his own unit. Such a convenient arrangement failed to materialise for the remainder of Lewis, and most individual crofters actually refused to accept the gift of ownership. The few who did acquired the name 'Free Gifters'.

# *Chapter 8*

> They are going out for their good and probably the old country does well not to judge them.
>
> The Scotsman, *23 April 1923*

The first quarter of 1923 was a period of intense activity throughout Lewis, with final preparations being made for the April departure. Shops did a roaring trade in suitcases, an advance posse of officials worked on the documentation and the occasional syndicate journalist would appear, to send back his report on just what it was, exactly, the Ontario Government had found.

As has previously been recorded, the general economic situation was bleak and, according to the *People's Journal,* worst of all in Ness, where many 'listless children' were 'half-nourished arid half-clad'. In fact, the country diet of fish, potatoes, oatmeal and dairy products was extremely healthy, but infant mortality was high, and many families had lost fathers in the war. In times of poor fishing or a bad harvest these families found themselves in difficulties. In 1923, a school medical officer reported:

> The present year shows that more children are below the weight average (than) for many years. This follows after the fact that there was in the last two years more children above the average than usual. That is to say the nutrition has been affected by- the bad harvest, the loss of employment and failures of tweed and fishing industries.

Those who had reached adulthood, however, formed an impressive body of men. 'Big, shy, likeable fellows,' said the *Journal*, 'with frank, open features and quick intelligence.' Or, as an (unnamed) emigration agent who handled overseas drafts at Glasgow remarked:

> When I look at these Hebrides men beside the others, I am proud to be a Highlander. They look as if they were capable of taking the others in their teeth, and shaking them.

In fact, preference was intended to be given to taller men (at least 5 feet 9 inches, and 12 stones in weight), and such physique, the

*Journal* representative (a Mr Chalmers) thought, was 'worthy of the race of giants from whom it is fabled they are sprung'.

The fact that this well-educated race of giants had only previously received the attention of the press when forced to engage in land raids seemed unworthy of comment although he *was* able to prognosticate that the islands would 'go back to the sheep farms and replace the clachans'. In the opinion of this scribe, the returning soldiers were already 'learning the futility of the patch of land and eventually, as they are beginning to do now, they will leave it'. Were the same man to visit Ness today, he would be most surprised by the evident prosperity of the large, rural population.

Early in the year it had also been announced that another emigration was to be arranged for the people of Barra and South Uist, although it would differ from its Lewis counterpart in a number of respects. Firstly, it was sponsored by an American Benedictine priest, Father Roderick MacDonnell ('the Moses of the Highlands'), via the Federal Government of Canada. Secondly, it would involve families rather than single men and women. And, thirdly, these emigrants were headed farther west, to Red Deer in Alberta. The *Metagama* had carried Barra emigrants before, but on this occasion the ship delegated was the CPR liner *Marloch,* and the fact that it was scheduled to leave Lochboisdale on 14 April 1923 – one week before the *Metagama* was due in Stornoway – merely served to heighten the Hebridean emigration fever which was about to grip the national press.

The *Metagama* was scheduled to reach Lewis on Saturday 21 April. It would pick up passengers at Glasgow the previous day, then sail to Stornoway, anchoring just outside the harbour on account of its size, with the SS *Hebrides* acting as tender. For a number of days prior to the sailing there was great excitement on the island. In Stornoway on the Monday there was a whist drive at the RTC Hut on North Beach, and a dance at the Masonic Hall. At the United Free Church the previous day, the Reverend Alex White chose his sermon from Genesis 12:

> And Jehovah said unto Abraham, get thou out of thy Country and from thy kindred and from thy father's house unto the land I will show thee.

Since the exact sailing time was uncertain, most of those from the outlying districts chose to travel to Stornoway the previous evening.

The SS *Metagama*, off Lewis (Courtesy Stornoway Harbour Commission)

The buses, according to the *Scotsman*, were 'motor vehicles of an antique pattern, with box-like open wagonette bodies, seldom seen elsewhere', while others came by horse and cart and some, even, on foot, with kists on their backs. Eighteen people were said to be going from the village of Sandwick alone, and a Mr Turpie, the local photographer, was the busiest man in town.

The *Gazette*'s editorial position had been made clear in the previous months. On 15 February it stated '. . . it is a standing reproach to our own Government at home that no room or opportunity for our young life can be found on the soil of our native land', and later, it stressed that it did not blame people for taking advantage of opportunities: 'They go by necessity, not for choice.'[1]

On the Friday night, the streets of Stornoway were thronged and it seemed to many that the whole island was there. Again, to the *Scotsman*, 'Roads into Stornoway resembled scenes of refugees fleeing before an advancing army', and the *Glasgow Herald* poignantly added that 'the element of compulsion was not entirely absent'.

Overnight, a keen north wind blew and the morning broke 'with a lash of rain'. The *Hebrides* arrived at 8 a.m., bringing six men from South Uist and five from North Uist, and by then the sun was shining, although the morning remained cold, at least until the big ship was sighted, just after 10 a.m.

The *Metagama* dropped anchor roughly a mile from the pier and soon the *Hebrides* was alongside, ready to bring off the Board of

The Territorial Pipe Band (Courtesy Norman McKenzie)

Trade official who was to make the final medical inspection. One of the large sheds on the pier had been set aside for this purpose. The liner had picked up more than a thousand passengers at Glasgow, plus 'a score' of journalists and cameramen (35, actually), and the media-men came ashore at Stornoway.

What greeted them, in the midst of a large crowd, was 300 'young men with sunburnt faces and new suits'. The emigrants were also distinguished by maple leaf badges, and when they filed through the shed for inspection, only one man was turned away.[2] The remainder emerged from the other side, and friends were crowded behind a roped-off area which gave passage to the *Hebrides*. The Territorial pipe band played and girl guides helped carry the luggage of female travellers. Each emigrant received a Gaelic Bible, and many touching departure scenes were perceptively recorded by, among others, the *Scotsman*: 'The eyes of the girls eagerly scrutinise the face of their youthful knight-errant who is going out into the great world, as if to photograph an impression of him on their memories.' Further on it reported: 'There is one young lad who scarcely looks the age limit of 18. The only one seeing him off is a younger sister.'[3]

The large crowd gathers round the tender – SS *Hebrides* (Courtesy Norman McKenzie)

The *Metagama* had been piloted into the harbour by Angus MacLennan, and the first Lewis man and woman aboard were Malcolm Graham and Maggie Kennedy of Garrabost. The first contingent also included town councillors, representatives of the Harbour Commissioners, ministers and other townspeople and they sailed from the pier (around 1 p.m.) accompanied by a flotilla of small boats. Once on board, the guests were given lunch by the Canadian Pacific Company, with ship's Captain Hamilton and Major Duffy, the company's agent in Scotland, presiding. Unfortunately, the major's speech demonstrated a rather scanty knowledge of Lewis history, saying that he hoped that this would be the 'first of many milestones in the march of emigration from the Western Isles', but he did follow this up with an appeal to pressmen to publicise the island's need for an improved mall service.

Captain A. M. Fletcher, Chairman of the Harbour Board, then welcomed the vessel and Baillie Stewart spoke on behalf of the town council. His colleague, a Councillor Mrs Gray of Sandwick, was to accompany the party to Canada. Mr Noxon spoke for

(Courtesy Norman McKenzie)

(Courtesy Norman McKenzie)

The last step . . . (Courtesy Norman McKenzie)

Ontario, saying that to any man in good health a future in Canada was assured, and the speeches were rounded off by a minister's Gaelic prayer.

Major Duffy then conducted the party through the ship. 'The cabins', said the *Journal,* 'each have four berths and the appointments in which the emigrants are travelling are very little inferior to those of cabin-class passengers.' Furthermore, 'everyone was happy', and the stewards served tea.

Meanwhile, the second and last contingent had been processed and the *Hebrides* ferried them to the liner around 4.30 p.m., to the strains of *Highland Laddie.* When this last group had come on board, the whole of the Lewis company was assembled on the quarterdeck and addressed in Gaelic by the Rev. Roderick MacLeod, F. C. Garrabost and the Rev. F. J. MacLeod, F. C. Ness. Gaelic psalms had been sung on the pier and the final address was evidently equally moving.

It was after six when the coaster and liner parted company and the *Metagama* remained within the harbour limits until 6.30 p.m. Some of the crowd had drifted home by then, but the bellow of the

Departure of the SS *Metagama* (Courtesy Cassells, Publishers)

horn brought many back to the sea front, and James Shaw Grant has described the scene:

> On the north shore the heather was burning and the fire smell came drifting across on a quiet wind to the *Metagama* as she swung round and steamed slowly out to the open sea. Then she bore to the east and then slowly to the north and soon we lost her behind the point.

Beacons were actually lit right round the north shore[4] and the last recorded message was from a neighbour of Donald 'Tulag' MacLeod of Ness. As boys they had played with torches, flashing messages to one another in morse code. As Donald watched the Butt of Ness from the ship, he saw a light flashing in code which he knew to be coming from his friend. 'What ship?' the flashlight requested. Donald doubted whether she would reply. Some time later his friend confirmed that the liner did indeed respond. The reply was 'SS METAGAMA and GOODBYE'.

* * *

Once the ship had gone, it was not only questions concerning emigration which lingered in Lewis. There was also the small matter of payment of harbour dues. When the Harbour Commission

The large crowd which saw off the emigrants from Glasgow's Princes Dock (Courtesy *The Bulletin*)

One of the flotilla of small boats whch sailed out to the SS *Metagama* (Courtesy *The Bulletin*)

bill was finally presented to Murdo MacLean as local agent for Canadian Pacific, it was calculated on the basis of sixpence per registered ton (net) and amounted to £191.8s.6d. – not an inconsiderable sum of money. Whether the matter had not been given prior consideration by the steamship company is open to conjecture, but the request for payment was met with prevarication by MacLean, who then wrote to the Minister of Transport for guidance on the commissioners' entitlement to impose such dues. The commissioners themselves were in no doubt arid, following another communication from MacLean in which he informed them that Canadian Pacific could not 'see their way to meet the Commissioners' account for dues' until they were in a position to 'prove that they are legally liable' they (the Harbour Commissioners) resolved to take legal action if payment was not forthcoming 'within fourteen days'.[5]

Within ten days Canadian Pacific themselves had entered the fray and, in a letter, claimed that:

> it was understood from the meetings which had taken place prior to the *Metagama* proceeding to Stornoway that the Harbour dues, if any, would be a trifling amount and before making such payment they were desirous of ascertaining particulars of the Schedule under which the charge was levied.[6]

The Harbour Commission, however, by then felt that they had satisfied the Board of Trade on this subject and, as a consequence, were fairly sure of their ground. Their secretary was instructed to enquire 'with whom the "meetings" referred to in their letter were held'.

Obviously there had been no official consultations with the harbour authorities on this matter, and if CPR had received any advice at all it was probably only the personal assurances of Murdo MacLean. It placed the company in a quandary, for CPR had plans

A prayer on board, prior to departure (Courtesy *The Bulletin*)

A eightsome reel, prior to departure (Courtesy *The Bulletin*)

to send more emigrant ships to Lewis and could not risk a souring of relations.

In October 1923, Murdo MacLean was instructed to offer a 'donation' of £50 to the Harbour Commission, without admitting liability or 'treating it as a precedent'. This was rejected, and a further claim for the full amount pursued. By February 1924 MacLean was offering £80 and a 'similar amount' for the SS *Marloch,* which was due on 26 April. Ex-Provost Smith moved that the commissioners compromise by offering to accept 50 per cent of the claim and, following an unsuccessful amendment by J. McR. Robertson that the £80 be accepted, the 50 per cent motion was passed by five votes to three.

The minutes of the Stornoway Pier and Harbour Commission record on 11 March 1924 that a letter had been received from Mr Murdo MacLean intimating that he had permission from the

Canadian Steamships Ltd to pay 50 per cent of the dues claimed and enclosing a cheque for £95.14s.3d. in full settlement. It further requested that some definite arrangement be made in respect of the SS *Marloch* and, to this, the commissioners applied the same compromise – i.e. 50 per cent of the Schedule Rate of 6d. per ton on the net registered tonnage. On 6 May 1924 it was further agreed to offer the SS *Canada* of the White Star Line a similar deal.

## *Notes*

1. Similar questions were publicly raised by Emmanuel Shinwell (Lab. Linlithgow) in the House of Commons; by the Highlands & Islands Committee of the Free Church; by the Scottish Home Rule Association; and the *Daily Sketch*.
2. The man, a native of Laxdale, was apparently rejected for an infection of the eyes. The story has given rise to an excellent anecdote from J. S. Grant. See 'Too Tall for Canada' in J. S. Grant, *Surprise Island* (James Thin). See also Note 4.
3. This was probably, Murdo MacFarlane (Melbost), a cousin of the Melbost bard of the same name and who, at 16, was the youngest of the emigrants. He was seen off by his younger sister, Mary, who later joined him in Canada. See Interview, Part III.
4. J. S. Grant, in *Surprise Island*, also mentions the story of Hector MacInnes – 'Noah' – of 44 North Tolsta, who instructed his friends to set fire to his thatch as the ship passed the 'Traighe Mhor'. There is, however, no Hector MacInnes named among the passengers of the *Metegama* so it was probably the *Marloch* or *Canada* from which he witnessed this symbolic gesture in 1924. See 'Funeral Fire at Tolsta' in J. S. Grant, *Surprise Island* (James Thin).
5. Harbour Commission Minutes, 14 August 1923.
6. Harbour Commission Minutes, 11 September 1923.

# *Chapter 9*

The heavy rolling of the ocean-going liner is naturally different from the quick, rocking movements of the fishing boats to which the Lewismen were accustomed, and many were seasick for the first two days. In spite of this, Mr Chalmers of the *Journal*, who had now been delegated to travel with the party to Ontario, reported that all were in excellent spirits. A Gaelic concert was given in the messroom on the Tuesday, and the Thursday brought a Gala Day and Highland Gathering on deck. There was a storm on the third day, but in spite of this the ship was making good time, and if the reported ice grip over the St Lawrence River had sufficiently relaxed to allow the steamer to get through, she was expected to reach Montreal on the Sunday or Monday – a total journey time of eight or nine days.

A number of characters emerged in the course of the voyage. Monty Montgomery, the tireless piper who is mentioned in the introduction and whose ocean-going performances are still warmly remembered by surviving emigrants; an exhuberant party of Fifers; a Salvation Army Group from Shetland; and even a contingent of Russian Poles, Letts and Jews, who were also travelling steerage[1] and reportedly fleeing Bolshevism. Food, however, was 'good and plentiful' and the talk was 'not of the past, but of the future'.

On the night of 27 April (nine days out), the engines stopped and there was a 'rush of escaping steam'. Those who hurried on deck saw ice floes 'of every fantastic shape' crowding in on the ship and a 'purple-tinted expanse stretching as far as the eye could see'. The *Metagama* was, unfortunately, in pack ice and movement was only possible at three knots with frequent stops, as the propeller blades became crowded by the floating masses.

On Sunday the 29th it was announced that it would be impossible to make Montreal by the proposed route. It was eight days since the ship had heaved anchor and they were now in the Gulf of St Lawrence, north of Cape Breton. On board there was said to be disappointment, since the alternative port of arrival –

St John, New Brunswick – had the reputation of being a slightly outlandish port, and the contingent of brides, presumably from Lowland Scotland, would now be married in the 'unlucky' month of May. In fact, the people of St John welcomed them warmly.

Naturally there were a great many more ships affected by the bad weather – a vast tonnage, in fact, of around twenty steamships. The *Marloch* (from Lochboisdale) was diverted to St John, and arrived on Saturday 28 April, five days behind schedule, and the *Montcalm,* which left the Clyde on the same day as the *Metagama* left Stornoway, was sighted en route to the same port. The SS *Canada* which, along with the *Marloch,* would visit Lewis the following year, was meanwhile diverted to Halifax. At one point, a three-masted schooner was spotted, which served to remind everyone of the hardships endured by previous emigrants, and boredom and frustration were held at bay by some official entertainment – a Highland ball and moving picture exhibition for cabin class; boxing exhibitions and a jazz band for steerage. And, of course, Monty played on.

On the bright spring morning of Wednesday 2 May 1923 – 11 days after leaving Stornoway and 12 from Glasgow – the *Metagama* sailed into St John Harbour. Two black-and-white tugs from the quarantine station at Partridge Island pulled alongside and doctors came aboard. The immigrants duly filed past them, and when the yellow quarantine flag finally came down around midday, the liner moved on to the wharfage at No. 4 Sand Point. The *Montcalm* was in the next berth, having arrived the previous day, and her passengers crowded on to the decks to welcome the *Metagama*. 'Good Old Rangers' was apparently one of the more esoteric greetings.

St John was well equipped to take large ships – work under construction was soon to make it the largest deepwater port in the world – but the volume of passenger traffic was unexpected and, to make matters worse, some of the streets of the town were under water. Melting snow in New Brunswick and Maine, USA, had caused the worst flooding for 50 years, and this had also brought havoc to the railway system. As a result there was no civic welcome and the Hebrideans and others did not clear the vast immigration sheds on the wharves until late afternoon. They were expected to get away on one of five special trains, but when this became uncertain owing to flooding they simply took advantage of their extended stay to view the city.

'Parties of sightseers', said the St John *Daily Telegraph*, 'could be found all over the city. Union Street, on the west side was crowded all evening and the store in that vicinity did a rushing business. One confectionery and fruit store almost cleared everything off the shelves to satisfy the visitors.'

On their first night in the New World, the *Metagama* passengers returned to the ship in order to allow the *Montcalm* people to proceed – via West St John Station – on the northern CNR route to Montreal. On the Thursday morning a train also managed to get into St John and, much to everyone's surprise, it incorporated the official Ontario Government coach carrying Manning Doherty, among others. The Minister of Agriculture had travelled 600 miles through bad weather to welcome the Gaels personally and he addressed them in one of the immigration halls. 'You are all young and inexperienced in the ways of this country,' he said. 'At the end of the year you will have learned many things about our methods which will prepare you for the future I have planned for you. The next year will be your apprenticeship period and, at the end of that time, those who have proved their mettle will be settled on a farm of 160 acres, and provided with stock on the repayment system by the Government.'

The speech was perhaps not the most inspiring ever heard, but the man had travelled for 36 hours in the midst of election preparations, and he was heartily cheered. What Doherty was talking about, said the *Journal*, was 'the croft on a scale unimagined' and Chalmers was further moved to comment that he had 'rarely seen such an open display of enthusiasm among men from Lewis'.

The scenes were again filmed, by Movietone News and the Ontario Government, and soon 13 coachloads of *Metagama* men and women were loaded up and on their way. A few miles out of town, however, the heavy coaches jarred to a halt and news that the Kenebaccasis tributary of the St John River had burst its banks and flooded the southern (CPR) railroad sent them back to the seaport.

Thursday night (spent on the train) wore into another day, and with frustration at every turn. Each meal, for example, required ten consecutive sittings and ever increased the possibility of a food

Murdo 'Monty' Mongomery at West St John Station, New Brunswick (Courtesy D. C. Thomson, Dundee City Library)

shortage. Milk had already run out. There was an obvious need for diversion, and it came in the form of a visit to the Imperial Theatre, the largest in St John. The manager – a Mr W. H. Golding – had evidently seen the possibility of publicity for himself and his theatre and invited the Hebrideans to a special picture show.

By now, Monty Montgomery was the star of all such occasions, and, in columns of four, everyone lined up behind the Laxdale piper and marched through the streets of St John. Windows and doors were soon opening along the route, and had it not been wet, said Mr Chalmers, 'the whole town would have been summoned'. Once inside, the party occupied the lower floor and, following some confusion regarding smoking and the wearing of hats, there were the obligatory speeches (Mr Doherty now spoke on behalf of the Hebrideans) and eventually some films: the arrival of the Prince of Wales at St John; a Larry Semon comedy; and a western serial. The main feature was Sir Hall Caine's *The Christian*.

The official Government party included George Patton, director of the motion picture publicity department, and his operator Roy Tash, who were themselves making a thousand-foot reel of film of the Hebrideans' journey; Mr MacDonnell, Director of Colonisation; R. S. Duncan, chief of the Agricultural Department; Mr Tutt of the Immigration Department; and Major Goodliff. There were also a number of newspapermen: Mr Van Passen *(Toronto Star)*; Mr MacIntosh *(Toronto Telegram)*; and Mr MacArthur of the *United Farmers' Journal*. A Mr Walters, secretary to the UF Party, completed the official line-up, and a fine time was had by all!

The Friday night was spent on the *Montcalm*, as it apparently offered better accommodation, and the last CPR train – that carrying the Lewis contingent – finally cleared St John at 6.20 on the Sunday morning. The massive pine forests must have seemed unwelcoming at first, but as the train entered rural Quebec, there were many railway stations with familiar names. Megantic . . . Sherbrooke . . . ah yes, the Leosach had been here before and, on that first Sunday, the Gaelic Bibles would not have been intrusive travelling companions.

Next morning, at Outrement railroad yard in Montreal, the train was brought to a temporary halt, and its occupants turned out. Once again, to their surprise, there stood on a raised piece of

T. B. MacAulay (left) and Manning Doherty greet the immigrants in Montreal (Courtesy D. C. Thomson, Dundee City Library)

ground Mr T. B. MacAulay, grandson of a Lewisman and president of the giant Sun Life Assurance Company, of which his father had been a founder. Flanked by Manning Doherty and the gaily bedecked president of the Montreal Caledonian Society, MacAulay proceeded to give the Gaels a welcome – and a pep talk. 'Save every cent you can,' was his advice. 'That's the secret of success in Canada. Once you get the capital, you are made.'

MacAulay did much in his lifetime for the Isle of Lewis and later gave many young Scots opportunities within his company which they would not otherwise have had. One (contemporary) Leosach has described him as 'making Lord Leverhulme look like a piker' (i.e. a shy person who is sometimes slow to find his wallet!).

After half an hour of this, the Hebrideans re-embarked and the initiative of one thoughtful Canadian official who handed round some bags of peanuts was praised by Mr Chalmers as introducing the Gaels to a great American novelty. He omitted to say that this was all they had to eat since they left St John.

## Note

1. Steerage was third class travel.

# Chapter 10

The legend of the *Metagama* and her Hebrideans had gone before them. For reasons which are still not absolutely clear, this emigration probably received more publicity than any other before or since.[1] Certainly the founders of two of Toronto's daily newspapers, the *Globe* and the *Telegram* were Scots, and the founder of the *Telegram* had Lewis connections. The fact that the Ontario Government chose to film the event also suggests that the introduction of Hebridean stock at that point in time had particular significance for a farmers' party about to go to the polls.

For whatever reason, this particular batch of 'quaint Hebrideans' was front-page news for weeks prior to their arrival in Toronto. The coming 'race of giants' theme was popular and recurring, and the *Toronto Star* – Canada's biggest selling newspaper – repeatedly reinforced the stereotype that if Hebrideans are quaint, then North Americans are daft.

> The historic and romantic Western Isles – where Saint Columbia [sic] who Christianized Scotland, made his home; where the clans of the MacLeods and MacDonalds had their origin – these isles are now being emptied. Only the old stay behind . . .'[2]

Unfortunately, some of the more insidious myths concerning the crofting communities were also crossing the Atlantic: 'Those who are getting State unemployment dole are almost the most affluent persons on the island.' There was also the occasional bizarre error. The *Star* of 19 April 1923, for example, carried four photographs of Caithness, with captions like 'Wick, a fishing village not far from the Hebrides'.

*Star* columnist Henry Somerville, however, who was based in the UK and may have been in Stornoway, was able to inject a note of realism by pointing out that the exodus had been going on for years, but no notice had been taken of it until there was the unusual feature of CPR liners calling at Hebridean ports.

In the main, comment regarding the arrival in Canada was

# RACE OF GIANTS ARE HEBRIDEANS; 400 COMING HERE

## Men of Party Which Sailed Yesterday All Five Feet Nine and Over.

## FEAR DEPOPULATION

## Sheep Farms and Deer Forests Replace the Island Crofter.

By HENRY SOMERVILLE.

Special Cable to The Star by a Staff Correspondent. Copyright.

London, April 16.—The exodus from Hebrides commenced yesterday when 400 Islesmen with their wives and families boarded the C. P. R. steamer Marloch at Lochboisdale, the solitary port of the Isle of South Uist, to Canada.

This party is going to form the Hebridean colony in Red Deer, Al-

(Courtesy *Toronto Star*)

favourable, but not uniformly so. A Mr R. Laing (or Lairg) wrote to the Immigration Department in Ottowa, from Toronto:

> Before assisting Scots from the Outer Hebrides to come to Canada . . . observe what those who came from there 100 years ago have done for Canada and for themselves. Go to the island of Cape Breton and you will see men of fine physique, no doubt, but living in poverty and content to do so. Their asylums are crowded. They are absolutely unreliable citizens (with, of course, notable exceptions . . . ) and not to be compared with Lowland Scotch who are thrifty.

Others, naturally, tried to paint a more attractive picture, like Donald MacLeod of 145 Riverdale who wished to correct the 'erroneous impression' that the people of Lewis were a poverty-stricken race: 'Nobody was ever known to be near starvation so far as I have been able to find out.' Margaret MacLeod of Ferndale Avenue was 'thinking of going back'. 'When Major Matheson was in charge,' she recalled, 'everything was alright.'

The Lewis Society of Toronto was also active, and as the great day of arrival approached, public interest remained high. It was 5.30 on the sunless morning of Tuesday, 7 May 1925, when the CPR train carrying the immigrants pulled into Union Station, Toronto. 'They were met', said the Toronto Star, 'by 75 sombrely clad men and women', who had previously 'scurried up and down the track' as tension got the better of them, and the note of anti-climax was unmistakable as the reporter informed his readers that there were, in fact, 'not many six footers . . . mostly young men, aged 18–25, and of medium build'.

Alas, this was to be only the first of many disappointments for the good people of Ontario.

The Gaels themselves, however, were buoyant. There was a flurry of handshaking and a volume of Gaelic and laughter, although some stood silent, peering around them and staring at the blackened station roof. Their clothes immediately caught the eve of the reporter: 'Men dressed in heavy homespun clothing; many wore trenchcoats or the blue coats of naval men, in evidence of war service', and 'the majority had caps'. The women, meanwhile, who appeared from the final coach were described as sporting 'suits of gray, with that cut that seems so strange in Canada . . . Old Country tailoring'.

Arrival at Union Station, Toronto (Courtesy *Toronto Star*)

The Leosachs had not come for a fashion show, however, and, for the men, the first stop was the Carls-rite Hotel and breakfast – paid for by T. B. MacAulay. The women, meanwhile, were escorted to Walker House, also in Toronto, and the general atmosphere, according to the *Star* reporter, was one of keenness to be started. A few, he understood, did not intend to stay on farms, but the majority did, and at least two of the women – Bessie Rennie and Chrissie MacLeod – knew that their destination was a dairy farm near Oakville.

For the others, the future was more uncertain. Some had been canvassed at Outrement in Montreal by farmers from Glengarry, who were not officially party to the scheme. Some were headed north, for Owen Sound, on Lake Huron. Many, like Donald 'Tulag' MacLeod, would take the trip south-west towards London, Ontario. And one or two, like Angus MacDonald, were staying right where they were, at least until they could make enquiries about alternatives at a local employment bureau.

Lewis women on arrival at Toronto (Courtesy *People's Journal*)

A group of Lewismen in Toronto (Courtesy *People's Journal*)

By the end of that day – Tuesday, 8 May 1923 – the Lewismen and women of the *Metagama* were dispersed, and on the final leg of their journey.

* * *

Two weeks after their arrival, the Hebrideans were still in the news, but for the wrong reasons. 'Not one of them ever worked here,' was the emphatic denial of Mr W. T. Kernahan, general

RONTO, WEDNESDAY, MAY 9, 1923

VICTION QUASHED.
,000 FINE INVOLVED

SITTING MEMBER O
OF S. OXFORD B

U.F.O. Now Likely to
Liberal Candidate in
Party Fight

HEBRIDEANS ON WAY TO ONTARIO

(Courtesy *Toronto Star*)

manager of O'Keefe's Brewery, Toronto, to the suggestion that nine Gaels, brought out to work on Ontario farms, were being used as strikebreakers.[3] In this case, Major Goodliff was able to confirm that none of 'his' men were, in fact, on the brewery's books, but by then it was known that a number of Gaels had gone AWOL, and there was another bad omen the following week when the *Metagama* was in collision with a freighter on the Clyde.

The defections were a particularly serious blow to the United Farmers Party, and they fell from office a month later. Goodliff subsequently managed to find some men at the construction of the Niagara Falls Power Station, and some were known to be

Typical farm, southern Ontario (Courtesy Peel Archive, Brampton, Ontario)

Bolton, Ontario. Typical small southern Ontario town in the 1920s. (Courtesy Peel Archive, Brampton, Ontario)

at the grain elevators of Goderich, Lake Huron, but others had simply disappeared – vanished into the great melting pot of North America.

The Canadian Unions were up in arms and questions were asked in the Federal Parliament. A Mr J. C. Mitchell, the Dominion Immigration agent in Toronto, demanded that 'action be taken against the 50 members of the Ontario party who took a passage loan but did not stick to the agreement'. And a Mr Little, the Ottowa commissioner, added that if the agreements were 'sufficiently specific, the Director of Colonisation might consider court proceedings'.

Donald MacDonald, Stornoway, cutting logs on his farm, Meadowvale, Ontario (Courtesy D.C Thomson, Dundee City Library)

Mr Chalmers of the journal then joined the chorus of indignation and wrote of the 'shame' which the defectors had brought upon their families back in Lewis, but, in the event, nothing was done. Obviously the men had no money and so it was pointless to sue – even supposing their agreement constituted a contract. The only realistic course of action was deportation – assuming they could find the men in the first place – and eventually this, too, was rejected, since it was generally agreed that to have them working somewhere in the Canadian economy was better than not to have them at all.

Of course, most of the immigrants did find their way to the farms[4] and stayed for periods ranging from a few days to a few years, depending on the treatment they received and the availability of alternatives. Also, in the main, farmers were happy with the labour which came over from the British Isles. It must be said, however, that the only official reports which specifically mention Hebridean workers tend to be rather negative.

> A considerable number, however, were sent to the County – a number from the party from the New [sic] Hebrides. These men proved very

> unsatisfactory and none remained in the district for any length of time, which gave the matter a bad knock.[5]

It couldn't have given the matter too bad a knock, because the emigration scheme was repeated by the Ontario Government the following year although, sometimes, the results were the same:

> At least 96 per cent of the men were from the British Isles and, with the exception of those from the Hebridean Islands, were a very good type of agriculturalist.[6]

There were, however, reasons for this disaffection and these are explained by the surviving emigrants themselves, in Part 3.

## *Notes*

1. The 1920s witnessed more Scottish emigration than any other decade – 300,000 people, most of whom went to Canada and the US.
2. *Toronto Star*, 16 April 1923.
3. *Toronto Star*, 22 May 1923.
4. Mr Chalmers of the *Journal* interviewed three men at work on farms outside Toronto. Donald Mackenzie and Murdo Cameron were working near Brampton, and Donald MacDonald in Meadowvale. All expressed satisfaction with the conditions.
5. Agricultural Representatives Annual Reports (MS597) Dufferin County, December 1923.
6. Report of the Minister of Agriculture (Colonisation and Immigration Branch), Province of Ontario y/c 31.10.24.

# *PART III*

# *INTERVIEWS*

# *Author's Note*

Not everyone I spoke to sailed on the *Metagama*. Some travelled on the *Marloch* or *Canada*, some went just before or just after the 1923/24 emigrations, and one is a Canadian who was growing up in New Brunswick when the *Metagama* arrived. Their different standpoints, I feel, help give a more complete picture of the time.

There are, by my reckoning at the time of writing, less than ten *Metagama* emigrants still alive in different parts of the world, and the fragility of their number was underlined when one man – James Ross MacLeod, formerly of Tong – died during correspondence with me. I managed to locate eight survivors and personally interviewed three, before augmenting their reminiscences with those of other emigrants.

In general terms, the men appear to have outlived the women – although men were in the large majority, initially – and Niseachs (people from Ness) have proved the greatest survivors!

Every attempt has been made to record the natural speech of the interviewees, although it should be remembered that Gaelic is their first language, and I am indebted to *Comunn Eachdraidh Nis* (Ness History Project) for the use of three Gaelic interviews with *Metagama* men.

The appendices which follow the summary record something of the song tradition which grew up around the emigrations of the 1920s. Morag MacLeod, Donald Archie MacDonald, Maggie MacKay and Margaret Bennet, all of the School of Scottish Studies, Edinburgh, were helpful in this area, and Donald J. MacLeod, Bridge of Don, kindly lent me some family heirlooms.

# *Donald 'Tulag' MacLeod*

*Detroit 1986*

I WAS BORN in Ness in December 1901 at 8 Knockaird. I had one brother and two sisters. My father and mother worked on the croft.

Before World War I, what's fresh in my memory is that my father left to go to the war, and we were left. I was the eldest, twelve years old. The others were infants. We had a croft and my father used to grow some beef for selling . . . and we had all that on our hands and my mother was pregnant with the youngest one. So we had very difficult times. This is fresher in my memory. And the whole responsibility of the croft was thrown on me at a young age. I left school – in Lionel – sooner than I should have and so the emphasis was not on education. There were a lot of things that I could have gone into under normal circumstances but the schoolmaster had nothing on his mind but the war. He was that type of person. And I was fairly high in my grades, but when I came to grade six – you could go to grade eight in Lionel at that time – he didn't learn us anything beyond that, to prepare us for life in any way. Because he was always talking about the war and nothing else. And he would ask where my father was, and so on. That generation was not actually prepared for anything.

Now, when the war was over . . . the war to end wars, as you remember, there was no more need . . . the military was discontinued. The Naval Reserve – that continued later on but during that period [there was nothing]. I was 17 when the war ended and my father came home in the spring of 1917. I wanted to go to work outside of the croft because there was no future in the croft as far as I could see. I had worked it as a very young boy and all we could get out of it . . . it was alright in its own way, we would never starve but all it would do was feed the family. During wartime and other times that was a blessing too, you know. We would never starve and we had eggs, poultry, and all that. But when the war ended I had no place to go. There was no work of any kind. After the war was over, the industry – before it got converted – was all geared for war work. There was nothing. Very little fishing. My father had some nets but they rotted there. There was some of the older generation fishing at the Ling fishing . . . but there was no fishing on the east coast, where a lot of the Lewismen used to go. The Government took over all the trawlers and the drifters and converted them.

I would go to Stornoway occasionally, sometimes with a horse and cart, and I had a cousin in Sandwick – a first cousin – that I used to go and see occasionally. Perhaps at certain times of the year I used to go over to her, doing this and that.

I worked for Lord Leverhulme, on the Ness-Tolsta road. I was gettin' ninepence an hour because I wasn't 18 yet! [laughs] The wage there was a shilling an hour. I wasn't old enough for that but I was doing the same type of work as the adults were. The work was very welcome to our way of thinking – we thought that bringing some kind of industry to Lewis would help . . . but the problem was that land was scarce in Lewis and there was quite a number of villages that were cleared away, and they were converted into sheep farms like Melbost and Galson. But they were promised when they would return from the war that these farms would be brought back to their original condition and divided into crofts. And Leverhulme was against this. But, especially the people in Back, they raided the place against his wishes, and then he stopped the whole thing.

Well, we had a croft . . . I didn't want a croft [laughs] . . . I didn't want nothing to do with it. I had so much of it in my schooldays that I didn't want to bother with it and we resented it, actually [the land raiding]. We sent people over to Back to see if we would come to some kind of compromise. But apparently it didn't. They raided the place and hence the reason that Lord Leverhulme . . . the whole thing came to a sudden stop. Now I was without a job again.

My father was back working on the croft. Now, the fishing days came to an end rather suddenly and he bought one of these large horses . . . to haul peat, and other materials. There was no buses at the time and all the commodities from Stornoway was coming by horses. And he bought one o' them and he was doing fairly well with it. Well, that horse was left to me and his customers were approaching me when I got to be about 15 or 16. Could I take my father's place and put in a day's work for them? Well, a day's work at that time came to about a pound a day which was

Donald 'Tulag' and Anne MacLeod, Livonia, Detroit, 1986 (Jim Wilkie)

extraordinary money. My father, before the war, was charging a crown, five shillings or something. This appealed to me. I was charging 18 shillings. I felt I was too young . . . I told them that I'd lower the price and do the same amount of work. [laughs] Eighteen shillings a day appealed to me. But when my father came, the horse, he said, was getting too old. So he bought another one – but at that time I had my mind made up, that I was going to leave the island, the first opportunity I had. A lot of the boys were worse off than I was – they weren't working at all. There were too many young men there for the opportunities that were present. People were keen to leave. The emigration was in the blood of the Lewismen going way, way back to the Hudson Bay Company . . . and then the railroad. Laying the tracks down from east to west . . . before my time.

The Church did not play a major role in my life before then, or long after it. I thought I was raised too strict – and I was glad to get away from the whole thing. It was years afterwards that I appreciated my background. That's common, but the Church had no influence at all on me. I wasn't heading in that direction at the time. Everybody went to church in the village, though. Nobody worked there on Sunday and we all went to Sunday School. And if you didn't go to church you were looked upon as an atheist, and so on. And if you had children that weren't baptised, you just didn't belong in the group. So, as far as religion is concerned we were just all in the same boat.

There was a man came to Lionel school – Major Goodliff (Murdo MacLean was the agent in Stornoway where we got our tickets) – and called a meeting. He worked for Canadian Pacific and told us of the opportunities in Canada . . . which didn't impress us that much. It was only $30 a month, and your board you were gettin' on the farm. Anyhow we felt it was a job and better than nothing, and the mainland was closed in our face because, if there were any opportunities at all, the ex-servicemen got it. We didn't, unless you were a professional of some sort. The Lord Leverhulme, yes, but not when you went to apply for a job sailing, which practically came to a stop for a short time after the war was over. And then the Naval Reserve began to recruit young men from Lewis, that was after I left. So that was the conditions generally throughout the whole of Lewis, as far as I can remember.

What I had in mind was coming to the States, because I read the history of this country during my schooldays. I read the history of the war between the states and I read the history of some of the battles. And the Puritans coming over here on the *Mayflower*. I was more interested in this country than I was in Canada. I didn't think Canada had much of a history at all. I still remember the Battle of Gettysburg and the young boy that impressed a Jewish doctor. He was dying there, wounded, a little drummer boy, 16-year-old, and he was taken care of by a Jewish doctor. And he told him to write his mother and say he was dying happy in the Lord, and Christ, and all that. And it impressed the Jewish doctor so much, he turned Christian. I was a lot more interested in this country – and at that time, Henry Ford began to appear in the press. I was gettin' the *News of the World* and he was asking also for labourers for Detroit. I had two uncles in Vancouver, but I had no desire to go out there at all. I was more interested in this country

[USA]. In fact, I liked Canada. It wasn't that different from my native island. And there was no crime. You could leave your doors unlocked at that time.

If others from Lewis didn't have the same idea then, they had it after they came to Canada. And one reason . . . they were only makin' $50 a month on the Canadian boats, while in this country they were gettin' $75, and a $100 for an able seaman. So the wage also was an incentive to cross the border.

Perhaps, in a way, the day the *Metagama* sailed was about the saddest day of my life. [laughs] Yeh. And one reason for that, regardless of what you go through, it was very very difficult for me to leave my parents and my younger sister. I was nine years older than her and I was more or less like a father to her because, when my father was in the war, I was the head of the household. And I felt responsible for them in many ways . . . and even when the war was over, they wouldn't mind my father, but if I looked at them it shook them up. [laughs] My brother was lost in the Second War. One sister is in Glasgow and another in Inverness.

I travelled the night before to Stornoway. We didn't know what time the *Metagama* would leave. We were told to be present at such and such an hour in the morning, because we had to get our papers in order, and all that kind of stuff. And we had to get lined up and there was no transportation that early in the morning, so we had to leave the night before. I came in a bus . . . they had buses then. Not too many, but some of the merchants, they bought buses because it became cheaper than a horse and cart. They could go over and get a load in an hour or so. What impressed me the most . . . and it was afterwards . . . if I spoke to any of the Stornowegians in Gaelic, they'd answer me in English. Of course, at that time, we were fluent English speakers – as fluent as they were. I met one of them in New York . . . I worked in New York for a while. And he was in the same boarding house with me and he used to come in and give me the *Gazettes* when he was through with them, and I usually spoke to him in English but he would answer me in Gaelic. Well, I told him one day – I says, 'I can't figure you Stornowegians out. If I spoke to you at home in Gaelic, you would answer me in English. Now, when I speak to you in English, you answer me in Gaelic. Why?' He says, 'I never appreciated my native language till I left home!' [laughs] I didn't really have that much acquaintance in Stornoway.

The impression was that they looked down upon those who came from the countryside.

What made the day sad . . . if I was goin' to the mainland I wouldn't have thought anythin' of it, but what made it sad for me . . . I knew I was on a one-way ticket. That I'd never come back. I never saw my mother again, or my brother. I saw my father and sisters. I was hoping to go home on a visit if I'd get enough money to do so, but when we were raising the family . . . we didn't have that much money. We couldn't leave 'em anyhow.

I remember the beacons very well. I saw them. I think most of them were on the west side and my next-door neighbour . . . we used to work the morse code with flashlights. And sometimes we used to talk to one another. We took up navigation in school. Three longs and two dashes . . . and I remember my next-door neighbour who was my pal . . . I knew that it was him who was tryin' to get in touch with the *Metagama*. And I saw his flashes . . . 'What ship?' I didn't know whether she answered. I didn't think she would ever answer. But he wrote to me and said that she did answer him, and the message was, 'SS *Metagama* and Goodbye'.

Most of us had no experience in the outside world at all. We ran into a storm, one time, and we had to heave-to. It was a very bad storm. I remember the waves coming in through the stern of the *Metagama,* and going all the way down on the decks. I remember that. Fairly bad storm. Then the ice. We saw icebergs at a distance, but not close . . . this was broken ice that we ran into. We were supposed to go to Quebec. They couldn't get through, so we went to St John. St John didn't impress me that much. We were a couple of days there . . . there was some kind of railroad that was washed out. Weather was so bad that no trains were running. We spent a night on the *Montcalm*. After we came off the *Megagama,* we couldn't leave St John. We went on the *Montcalm* and spent a night there. And then, I think, the other night we spent on the train . . . she stopped somewhere . . . but it was very uncomfortable.

I remember Monty [the piper]. He used to come in there and he always had a dram. He was always coming, swinging . . . he had the kilt on, too, you know? He was a big, handsome man, you'd think he was made for the kilt. He was older then we were. I saw the first black man in St John. [laughs] I was 21.

We arrived in Toronto very early in the morning and there were some in the railroad station, but I had no relatives at all. We took the train to London, Ontario, immediately and we stopped there . . . there was quite a few of us there . . . it was a kind of waiting room. And the farmers came in and they would pick someone and hire him to work with them on the farm. There was another boy with me from the same village, an Angus MacDonald. He's dead now. And there was one [farmer] there who wanted two – a dairy farm. So we went and hired out to the dairy farmer. No doubt they looked at the size of us. There'd be about 25 of us went to London. The dairy farm was owned by a doctor in Detroit – a Doctor Brady – and the foreman on the farm was a Mr Wight, who was an Englishman. He was one of these 'home boys' (i.e. from a home) that they used to send from England. There was a lot of English home boys they shipped to Canada. They had no parents. I would say he was in his early thirties. He was married and had a child. He'd been there in Canada before the war as a young lad. There was a house there on the place that he [the farmer] built for this man, and we were staying with him, and got our meals from him. We were always well treated. We never felt any discrimination of any kind. Although they were looking for cheap labour and they were bringing the home boys from England, mostly. I never met a home boy from Scotland.

There were 50 milking cows and I learned to run the milking machine – I'd never seen one before – and that was my job. He also had black men besides us. It was a 300-acre farm. Big farm. I had to get up at five o'clock in the morning and I had to go on horseback to round up the cattle – to milk them. Two dogs to round them up and I had to bring 'em in, and this black man, he used to set 'em up and both of us milked. I was quite satisfied there as far as that was concerned. I wasn't overworked, but the working hours were long. Dawn till dusk, and there was no recreation.

There's a town there – North and South Buxton – all black [people] in Canada. They were descendants of slaves that escaped across the river during the days of slavery, and the Canadian Government gave them a piece of land there, and it's still the same. He [the black farmhand] had a small house on the farm, too. The Canadians, all their help, they had houses on the farm. I got on fine with the black man . . . he was a real, nice man. He was an elder in the Baptist Church, a very religious man. And I got a scare, one day.

There was terrific electrical storms there . . . I had never seen anything like them. Thunder and lightning, and one of 'em hit close by one day and knocked the chimney down – I was tending the milk cows and opened the door and went to the stable – they don't call them 'byres', they call everything 'stables' whether it's horses, cattle – I got scared. Apparently the cows sense an impending storm, which we don't. And they were very unruly that morning. They wouldn't go in their own stalls. And I suppose I came up with a couple of cuss words. If a cow was in the stall, the other one that belonged there, she wanted to get in, too, you know? And when the thing was over, I was scared to death, the lightning came so close. And the black man looked at me and said, 'Are you afraid?' 'Yes, I am.' 'I don't see why,' he says, 'I heard you saying your prayers this morning!' That was a hint that I was cursing. [laughs]

They hadn't got anything like the modern machines that they have today, but they had a tractor and a hayloader. But it was mostly horses they had at that time. They had a reaper driven by horses, but that was about all. We had milkin' machines, of course. Easier to milk . . . run by compressed air.

I kept in touch with Lewis when I was there, but I didn't stay there very long. About two months. And then we got an opportunity to go commercial fishing, and that paid a lot more. We weren't *bound* to stay – we were free to go any place. On the farm we got a wage. We all had to take out a loan from the Canadian Government for our fares, and we had to pay that back. It was $90 (£16–£18) from Lewis to Toronto. We were expected to pay it back at so much a month, but we weren't gettin' that much. The wages were $30 a month. Now, I paid that back. I wrote to Toronto and told them that I left the farm . . . that I got about twice the money . . . about $60 or $75 for fishing . . . and that when the season would be over, I'd go up to Toronto and pay them, which I did. I was fishing on Lake Eric, down about, oh, 100 miles from Windsor . . . somethin' like that.

Most of the Lewis boys stayed a couple of months. See, most of 'em went sailing if they had the opportunity. I had an opportunity to go sailing and I didn't care too much for it. You were there seven days a week and it was six [hours] on and six off, or somethin' like that. You never had a day off, or anything. The fishing was similar to salmon fishing with cribs – catching everything from white fish, herring, bass, perch, sturgeon. They had what they called a 'leader'. When the fish would hit this barrier they would try to get around it and go into the trap. It was a trap net . . . and we emptied them every morning . . . all kinds of fish, working from a boat. They went quite a distance up into the lake. The cribs would start in shallow water but the nets were tapered as the water got deeper. Most of the fish ran in shallow water. The boats were flat-bottomed. Not quite as big as the drifters they had then in Lewis. And they would carry an awful lot. I liked Canada. Quite a bit like our own island except that they were better off than we were. I was never on the mainland of Scotland till I returned home. 1957. [laughs]

The lakes freeze over in winter time and we had a couple of months off and I crossed the river [Windsor–Detroit] then, as a visitor, to see what the climate was. There was a ferry. Neither the tunnel nor the bridge was built then. I think it was 1928 that the bridge was built. I would say I went on the ferry about 1926, and I found out in Detroit that we could pick up a job anytime, and nobody asked any questions, whether you were there legally or illegally. So I went to General Motors . . . and that was in Flint, about 60 miles from Detroit, and I just walked into a job. There was some other Lewismen there. The automobile industry was in its infancy at that time, and nobody wanted an ID. There was no social security or anything, and when I walked into the Employment Office, they didn't ask me any questions . . . didn't even ask where I was born. I found out afterwards that the girl who signed me up put me down as American-born. She detected an accent, but we all had accents. The Southerners had a different accent.

Going into General Motors plant was a sight! But I didn't stay that year. I went back again fishing for a summer. Then I put my name in to get in the country [US] legal. And I had a job lined up in General Motors. They had the assembly line going, but I was in the testing department, testing engines for any flaws. March 1928, my name came in. I had to put my name on the British quota. Although, automatically, you became a Canadian citizen at that time, I had to come in as a Britisher. There was no difference . . . coming to Canada or going to Glasgow. There was no ID, no passport or anything. So, as long as you were there, six months in one certain place, you could vote as a Canadian.

I voted a couple of times. One place I was in Canada during the years I was there, it was a Puritan-style community. Descendants of Highland emigrants that were cleared. They stuck to the Gaelic and to the customs of their parents, and they were against liquor. At that time, the United States were dry and Canada was supposed to be, but there was a lot of what they called 'bootleggin' – illegal drinking. So it came up to a vote one time in a certain community I was in, and I was eligible to vote. There was only one voted for liquor . . . and they thought that it was me! [laughs] But it wasn't. Bruce County, close to Southampton. I went back on a farm after the first year I was fishing in Canada, during the winter time. I didn't go to the States then, but I went up to pay my [*Metagama*] fare there and it took all the money I had, almost. And then they gave me a job on the farm. After that, I came over to the States. But, generally, Canada was really nice.

I came into the States, permanently, in 1928 and became a citizen in 1935 (I also got married that year, to Annie Murray from Skigersta Ness). I got laid off at General Motors when the depression came, in 1930. You had no income, no work.

I went to New York and worked in a tunnel with a construction company. It was a water tunnel. They were bringing the water from some lake, way out in New York State. It was for city water (1930). And then the Holland tunnel was built before that. That was a different thing, going under the Hudson. Some Lewismen were killed there. Working in the tunnel was dangerous, but it was paying pretty good.

In the water tunnel, some died and many were injured. I didn't work down in the tunnel, I worked in maintenance. I was mostly on the elevator and we used to put up pipes to draw the foul air out. One fellow was telling me that those who shovelled down there, they called them the 'muckers'. They used to shovel rocks into the small railroad cars they had down there. They had tracks. And he was filling one of them and a big boulder came from the ceiling and cut the shovel in two. The other half of the shovel disappeared! He had only the handle in his hand. Well, he wouldn't go down there again. He says, 'I was four years in France in the First World War – I knew where the enemy was! This is more dangerous!' [laughs]

I was in New York not quite a year. I came back, I didn't like it, and I started work with another company in Detroit. One reason I didn't care for Flint, it was a General Motors town. If GM went down, there was nothing there.

Detroit had Ford, Chrysler and all that. Detroit was a very different place to the way it is now. Very little crime except amongst the gangsters, and they wouldn't bother you. You couldn't wish for a better neighbour. They had that 'rum running' at the time. Bringin' illegal liquor into the States. And if you got into their racket, they'd wipe you out. But apart from that, there was no crime. We raised the family in Detroit, and our door was unlocked. We weren't afraid of anyone. We were in an Italian neighbourhood. Some Germans. We sold that place in 1965. And then there was the riot, in 1967. That's when the whole thing began to deteriorate. Detroit, then, would become dangerous. So we bought another house in Detroit on the west side. It was closer to my work. I had a number of jobs with the same company. We worked on aircraft a little bit, before and after the war. We worked for an aircraft company in New Jersey and we were makin' part of a Navy jet. The section that was at the rear of jet planes on board the carriers. The same company I worked for, for 25 years. Then they closed the doors. Goin' out of business like a lot of them. I got a job with another company.

We were 25 years in the same house. Our children were never molested. No such thing as a break-in or robbery. It wasn't as safe in Glasgow as it was here. I don't know what happened. There's a lot of black people livin' downtown . . . but I wouldn't be afraid to go down there. The black kills themselves more than they do the white.

I was in Lewis a couple of times, in '57 and '69, when I retired. I'm retired 17 years. [laughs] We had a very good life here. I wouldn't trade it for any place in the United Kingdom. And we got into this place [sheltered apartment]. I've been active in the Church since 1940. Our church here [Livonia] is connected with the Free Church.

## *Angus MacDonald (Ness)*

*Buffalo 1986*

MY FATHER AND MOTHER came from Ness . . . my father was a fisherman and my mother, in all her life, she never left the island. Both worked on the croft. There was eight [brothers and sisters] but the only one who came to manhood besides myself of the boys – he died when he was 17. Now, I had four sisters. Three of them was married and the fourth one was a twin, but she never was married. I went to Lionel school. In them days, unless your parents could board you in town, you couldn't go to Stornoway school – 27 miles away.

I was born, July 1900. There was two boys from our village in my memory, that went to the Nicolson. Their people could afford it. Now, everybody goes to the Nicolson, cos there's transportation. All I wanted to do was get out of school and go to work. [laughs] When you were able to do anything you worked on the croft. Well, when I was 14 – everybody left school at 14 – we got a boat, six of us, and we were goin' out fishin' and gettin' loads of fish every day – never sold any of it. The families that didn't have anybody to go out fishin', our mothers was givin' them the fish free . . . cos they couldn't afford to buy it . . . that's the way the village worked in them days. But it's different today. You have gotten money in the line today but there was no money in them days.

I was in the Royal Naval Volunteer Reserve, and I was workin' on a minesweeper, the latter part of the war. And, when the war was over, they asked for volunteers to sweep mines from the Belgian coast. So, I volunteered because they were givin' us double pay. And my father was sayin', 'Am I losing my only son because he's greetin' for money?' [laughs] So I told him – when the six months are over, I won't volunteer anymore. And you know six months back at home I tried to get back in the Royal Naval Reserve and they wouldn't take me . . . because they had to pay my fare from Ness to Stornoway. They discriminated against us.

I didn't go to Stornoway very often. I'd go there sometimes with my grandfather's horse, because I used to go and get loads for the merchant in the village. Sometimes I'd replace [my grandfather] and go for the load, once every couple of months. That was all I knew about Stornoway.

We never got Gaelic at school. All we got was English. In the playground, Gaelic was all we were talkin', but in the classroom, the only Gaelic was . . . the teacher would read a verse out of the Bible in the morning.

During the war, I was minesweepin' in the English Channel. We couldn't sweep at night – we were patrolling at night – and sweepin' in the daytime because if you sweep at night and a mine got away from you, you couldn't see it and it might hit one of your own ships. I volunteered without comin' home and they kept me in Dover, there, as a watchman . . . oh, for about a year. See, the minesweepers they had were fishin' boats . . . they were made of wood. And they'd repair them and send them back to their owners. So, every few weeks, one of them would be ready, and I was one of the crew. Goin' back again by train, we'd stay a night in London . . . for a lil' good time . . . before we'd go back to Dover again. All the fishing boats came from as far as you could get in Scotland . . . as far as Cape Wrath. We sailed them all around the coast and took a train back to Dover again. The skipper we had, he owned three of the drifters himself – him and his brothers. So, he wanted to have a good time in London because his wife was in Dover . . . and you know, when he'd go to the picture show, I was the youngest boy he had in the crew . . . he'd take me with him so his wife wouldn't get a chance to bawl him out for his drinkin'. [laughs] I'd be about 18 years old then. See, I joined when I was about 17 so that they wouldn't get me in the Army . . . they were killin' them like flies. Some of my buddies that was a year or two older than I was, they were all killed off. . . from Ness, all over the island. So that's why none of us in the end wanted to wait for the conscription. There was seven other guys that joined with me. We left the same day for the barracks in Portsmouth.

I went back to Lewis, probably 1920. I had a couple of years, but when I got back it was impossible to find work. So this Major Goodliff – he must have been workin' for both governments – he came to the schoolhouse. We had to go there and sign up . . . have a physical . . . and just wait till he got a shipload. I never worked for Leverhulme. See, when I came home from the Navy, I went to look

Angus MacDonald (right) with friends Ann and Joe Bernecky, Buffalo 1986. Ann's father, Charles McIver, was a founder of the Lewis Pipe Band before emigtating at the turn of the century. (Jim Wilkie)

for a job . . . workin' at the road . . . and they told me, 'Leverhulme is closin' down' . . . so I didn't get a job there. Boys that didn't leave home, they worked on the roads there, for Lever. There was only one more draft, after me, to be called up.

[When I was minesweeping] there was one with me from St John, New Brunswick. Canada was alright but, see, my uncles were in the United States and I wanted to go and see them. They were my father's brothers and, 1912, they came over to the CPR railroad, same as we came to the farmers. They kept on goin' till they got as far as Vancouver. From there, they emigrated to Seattle,

Washington. They got small wages and they were writin' back and forth. When I came over here, one of my uncles, he sent me some money to help me. He used to send my mother a couple of pounds every year. There was another one . . . a first cousin o' mine livin' next door . . . an' his father and mother could order anything they wanted from the shop, and he'd pay at the end of the year.

One [of my uncles] was workin' in the sawmill, the other was a carpenter. In Washington [State] there, it's great timber country and most of the bridges was built with timbers, so he worked there till the war started, then he went to Bremerden naval yard and got a job there as a rigger. The other one stayed in the lumber mill all the time, till he got so old, he couldn't. He belonged to the Masons and when he couldn't work any more, he went to the masonic home and he turned his home over to the Masonic Lodge. That was the payment. He didn't have any family.

The only way I could come [to America] was on this scheme [*Metagama*]. I didn't have any money to come any other way. So we all grabbed the chance at this scheme. There was nobody had money there [Lewis]. Not too many had relatives in this country, though.

There was a fellow from Ness . . . the day he went aboard [the *Metagama]* he got seasick, and he didn't eat one bite of food till he got to St John. He was taken off in an ambulance. Vomiting, and nothing to throw up. At the table where I was eating, when we got on board, oh, there'd be about 50 at the table. I seen some days there'd be only four. All seasick – I never got seasick!

I had sisters to see me off – oh, you should see the gang on the quay at Stornoway! Another fellow by the name of Monty [not Montgomery] was there with his bagpipe band. I think it was Monty MacLeod. Monty Montgomery only played on board the ship. He played in Cleveland too. He was a good piper . . . but he was a good drinker, too! [laughs] I seen two people holdin' him up on the dance floor!

Everybody was homesick . . . I remember when she was goin' by the Butt o' Lewis, well, they were blowin' the horn all the time, and everybody in Ness was out makin' bonfires. Even my father was cryin'. And we were on deck until we seen the last flicker o' the light disappear. So then we went down below, and – that's it. We never seen that light again. I never saw my mother or father again.

My father was a very religious man, he was always an elder in the church. We'd never go to bed without my father reading the Bible. And each one of us, when we got old enough to have a Bible, following him. That's how I learned to read the Gaelic.

When I saw the farms in Canada (from the train), that was enough for me. When I saw a team of horses, and one man. And land, nothing but land. I knew I couldn't work in a place like that. So there was no point in me tryin' it. I thought it was too much ploughing for me in the first place. I can't work like that. I wanted to be on the water. That was my life.

I decided I wasn't goin' to a farm. That's for sure. That's (because) I was the only one in our gang that was away from home before. I knew there'd be such a place that'd be hirin' labourers for someplace. There was three other guys with me. And they were from the same village I came from. Angus MacKenzie, John MacKenzie and Malcolm Morrison. So we went to an employment office in Toronto and I says to the man, 'I see you're lookin' for labourers. Well, that's what we're lookin' for . . . labour.' And in about an hour we were on the train . . . huntin' for Lewiston (Niagara Falls). But when we got there the camp was closed. We found a hut to sleep in but there were no bedclothes. So Malcolm Morrison and I climbed on to one mattress together, for warmth, and put another mattress on top. In the middle of the night there was a terrible thunderstorm and Malcolm said, 'Do you think it's the end of the world?' 'Well,' says I, 'I don't know. I've never been there!'

In the morning, before they'd give us any breakfast, some guy took us down to show us where we'd have to work. It was a cliff face (power station). He said, 'Can you work there?' 'Aye,' says I, 'we were after seagulls' eggs in worse places than that.' [laughs] So, then they took us back to the camp and we start eating. They were putting an addition to the power house. And they had to make a space there for a big pipe to let the water down from the canal above. See, the water was comin' from Niagara Falls through a canal and it was goin' through a pipe, down through the generators. And that was our job . . . to dig this hole so that they could put that pipe in the hole. Naturally, it was dangerous. That's why everybody wouldn't go there. And our boss was a French Canadian. And when we quit . . . he quit too! Next time I seen him he was in Buffalo and he called me from across the street, 'Angus, do you want to work as an iron rigger? You've got the nerve for it.' I says, 'I know I've got the nerve for it, but water is in my blood . . . I want to go sailing.' [laughs] So that's what I did. I think I would have got killed if I got a job there . . . I was too much of a show-off.

To get into the States, you had to have $200 pocket money, and $8.40 for head tax. We went in two at a time because we didn't have enough money for all of us to come over. When two got in legally, one of us went back with the money for the next two. We got a boarding house close to Falls Street [Niagara Falls, USA] and went out the following day looking for a job. We had three jobs to go to the following morning because at Niagara Falls then there was so much work, they couldn't get enough help. And my immigration was clear. All we could do was construction work.

Well, I worked in construction all summer long, and when it started gettin' cold, I got a job in a factory. It was an Englishman that was the superintendent and everybody workin' at the furnaces . . . they were Italians. He wouldn't give me a job like that. We were makin' the gravel to make sandpaper, and it was goin' in a barrel at the end of the conveyor. All I had to do was write two letters when I put the cover on a barrel, and nail this on. He gave me that job because I wasn't Italian, and the man that was in charge of the shippin' room, he was Canadian. But he was quittin' to go home, and the Englishman was givin' me the job in charge of the shippin' room. Small thing.

Next day, I took a railroad goin' to Buffalo. First thing I seen was three passenger ships, fitting out for the season. Right away I says to myself, 'That's where I'm gonna work!' So I went back to the Falls and quit my job. I was in Buffalo the following day and went down to the passenger boat. I asked for a job. 'Got papers?' 'British Navy.' 'They're no good here.' So they gave me the goin' over and I got my seaman's papers, AB papers.

'What do I need now?' 'A lifeboat ticket . . . [laughs] go over to that lighthouse, to the coastguard.' The first thing he asked me was, 'Can you row a boat?' There was chunks of ice in the harbour as big as this table. So I rowed around them and I skulled around. Back to the dock.

'Now you gotta tell me the provisions of a lifeboat.' 'Well,' I says,

Power station construction, Niagara Falls (Courtesy *Illustrated London News*)

'if I can't tell you in English, I can tell you in Gaelic.' He finally asked me, 'Where the heck did you come from?' 'Did you ever hear of the island of Lewis in the Hebrides?' 'I heard of it and I've seen it'. (He was over there during the war.) 'The best seamanship I ever seen was in that Minch. Them little fishing boats. You got your lifeboat ticket!' [laughter]

I was on the lakes every summer – on passenger boats – two years on each one. Then I went on a package freighter. We were carrying merchandise from Buffalo, and flour and cold storage from Duluth. From there I went on to the *Canadiana* – passengers to Crystal Beach. They had a riot on her between negroes and Canadian immigrants so, when she tied up, I got a job on an automobile carrier. Carryin' automobiles from Detroit to Buffalo . . . 450, 500 cars each trip – that was my last job sailing.

I worked on her for eight years. Whatever kinds of cars they were makin' in Detroit at the time, we carried them. We took them to Buffalo and a railroad picked them up. But the railroad put them out of business . . . they went to the plant, and loaded there. They didn't need boats any more.

We worked in Cleveland in the winters. The manager would give us a job after we got through sailing, but they got tired of this and couldn't promise us a job any more unless we promised to stay. Makin' Ever Ready batteries. So I got a job in Seattle, haulin' the salmon down from the canneries.

There were six canneries and we used to stop at each one comin' down. Canned salmon . . . and the crew had to handle all the cargo, because they had no longshoremen up there. We were goin' up with supplies, whatever they needed. I've seen some of us so tired, waitin' for the next load to come down, they'd hit the deck before the load did. All in. I seen me goin' to the wheel from one cannery to the other, and the mate would stand behind me. When he'd see me dozin' off, he'd shake me. He wouldn't take the wheel. That was my job. We would sail up to Alaska, drop the supplies, take the canned salmon, and drop them in Seattle.

Then I got sick for the Great Lakes again. And I seen a ship loadin' timber in Tacoma. She looked like a forest. All you could see was booms. It was the same thing. 'Have you got AB and lifeboat tickets?' First two days, I was standin' watch. Then the bo'sun, he picked me to work with him as a day man. I was all set.

We went through the Panama Canal with this load and we came up to Brooklyn, New York. And I had a suit – I'd got a new suit in Seattle – but I didn't have a lock for my locker. When I went to look for my suit, it was gone. So I had to go over to New York when I got off the ship. The mate wanted me to stay, take the bo'sun's job, but everybody was quittin' anyhow. I went to a second-hand store and got a suit that would take me up to Buffalo, so I wouldn't come in my overalls. I didn't see much of New York.

I was married in February 1942. I was 38 years old and Chrissie was four or five years older than me. She came from Carloway, but I met her in her parents' home in Buffalo. I was in a TB hospital for a year out in Parisburg 40 miles from Buffalo. They found spots on my lungs and they never gave me any medicine – they said sleep outside. In winter . . . right out on the porches. That was the only cure in them days. I remember wakin' up one night and when I tried to get out of bed, I couldn't, till I 'broke' the sheet that was on top of me. I had to break it because it was solid ice. 1940 or 41. The doctor says he can trace the TB yet. I went down to 75lbs when I was in the Marine Hospital. And they put the screen around me. And Broxy[1] was tellin' me, he says there were 30 [Lewis people] out on the lawn there, one day, waitin' to get the news that I was dead. Only two could get in at a time. Jessie Gillies went home. She was married then, and she says, 'I'll never see Angus MacDonald alive again.' They're all gone but the Broxy and me.

I didn't know Broxy at home. I met him in Buffalo. He stayed in Ann Bernecky's home. A lot of them stayed at the MacIver 'Boarding House'. A lot came to visit, and some stayed. It was a house you were looked after in, including me sometimes. Cheese and crackers, an' playin' cards. Help yourself. Yeh. Oh, that was a great home.

In the Marine Hospital I remember, one night, I didn't want to bother the nurse in the middle of the night. I wanted to see if I could make it to the bathroom myself. So, I was gettin' hold of the beds, and I made it, standing up. But comin' back I had to come back on my hands and knees. I couldn't stand. Still, I didn't want to tell the nurse about it. To me, America was the best country there was. Still is.

There was a friend of mine working at Irving Airshoot [Buffalo]. And they were looking for somebody that could sew canvas. So I

Great Lakes steamship (Courtesy Public Archives of Canada)

went up there and I got the job, but the first day I went in there with two black eyes. I was drunk the night before and my wife Chrissie was takin' me home, and I fell up against a tree. My nose hit the tree . . . two black eyes . . . the first day on the job. But I went there anyhow. There was a guy there, one of the bosses, by the name of MacLeod. He came and looked at me. 'Well,' he said, 'give him a chance. Maybe it was an accident.' They never seen me with a drink again. They made parachutes during the Second World War – this was after I got out of Parisburg – and they were makin' chairs for aeroplanes, too.

With the parachutes, there was a long table, and we folded up . . . I think it was ten 'chutes. Then we were takin' them twice in a week, out to the airport, to drop them with a dummy in –180lb solid rubber dummy. One of us would go up in the plane, see that everything was alright, and drop the dummy. There was two others on the ground. Then we would gather the 'chutes, take them to the hangar and drop them a second time. One day, one got away from the dummy and landed on top of the city hospital! Without the dummy! And the dummy came so close to the guys on the ground, it's a wonder it didn't hit them! It sank two feet in the ground!

Major Goodliff wrote two or three times later to my father. And my father ignored him. I think it was the third letter . . . I told my father, give him my address, so he'll leave you alone. But my father never wrote again. [laughs] What the MacIain went through in his life!

## *Note*

1. Broxy was Norman MacKenzie, also of Ness. See Interview No. 6.

## *Mary (MacFarlane) MacIver*

*Toronto 1986*

I WAS BORN on August 28th, 1909, at 9 Upper Garrabost. My mother was from Garrabost and my father from Melbost. I had two brothers and my mother died when I was five. She died of TB, a common disease in those days. My young brother was only two. We were sent to my father's brother in Melbost. He had a family of his own – Murdo (MacFarlane), the bard, another son and three daughters. And their mother was still alive. There was nothing in Lewis in those days.

I went to Knock school. We walked from Melbost, which was nearly three miles, in very bad weather, and if the rain came, and the spray from the ocean, you would be soaked by the time you got to school, and sitting in the wet clothes all day. They were very strict. It was a Mr Morrison who was the headmaster, then a Mr Burns. You couldn't talk to the kids, or anything. And the strap was there – not that we seen it used very often. Gaelic was the language of our home, and when we went to school we couldn't speak a word of English. But at school we didn't speak Gaelic. The teacher used to read a Gaelic chapter from the Bible, but all the rest was English. Although they didn't frown upon us using Gaelic amongst ourselves. You only went as high as standard six as we used to call it, at Knock school. So I suppose the parents couldn't afford to send us to the Nicolson Institute. They had to pay for the children to be in a private home. Paid the room and board and I believe today they don't even have to pay the bus flares. That worked against the country people. Very much so.

Every Saturday night was our outing and it was our big day. Walking . . . there would be all the boys and all the girls from the village of Melbost. We started off at six o'clock and we would walk up to the town. They would give us a few pennies before we left home, and that was our treat for the week. We would buy candy [sweets] and we got more kick out of that than you would for £10 today, I'm quite sure. There were no dances for us at that age.

I came from a very godly home. My uncle and my aunt were very godly people. There was a morning prayer and a night prayer, and we were raised something like that. And, do you know, I think of these days now – very often – and I think, well, what godly people there were in those days.

My father was on the sailing boats before the [First] War. He went to war . . . right through the war . . . and he died of war wounds after he came home. He only lived about a year after he came home, but we were so young, we didn't realise what happened. And we liked Melbost. My uncle and aunt, they were so kind to us. There was no difference made, although there were two families there. It's since I grew up that it bothered me. We were so young . . . we had, like, a new father and mother and we grew up with them. It was after I came out here [Canada] that I missed having a father and mother.

I remember when the *Iolaire* happened. The morning after, I remember a man coming into the house . . . to my uncle's house . . . and saying, 'A terrible thing happened last night.' And he mentioned the name of the boat, that it went on the rocks, and my father asked that man, 'Was my brother-in-law on the boat?' And he said, 'Yes, he was lost.' He came from Aird. I remember very well. And the men, of course, went up . . . round the beach, looking for their own, and the caps would be coming ashore. And the tunics. It was a very sad thing. A very, very sad thing.

When Leverhulme came to Stornoway . . . it's a very vague memory . . . but I remember the old gentlemen at home in the village. Some would be all for him and some would be fighting against him. And they didn't seem to agree on one thing.

Murdo, the bard, was my cousin. And I also had a brother called Murdo MacFarlane. I don't think I ever saw the bard that he didn't have a book in his hand. He would be in the bedroom, there, reading the book from morning till night, if there was nothing else to do, and he would be singing to himself quite a lot, outside. Around the back of the house, the barn, you would hear him singing and he used to go right down to the ocean, you know, and look out in the ocean, and he would be singing. He was ten years older than I. When he took ill, when he wasn't able to look after himself, he went to live over in Tong. Our relations over there asked him to go over, and they would look after him, because one of the daughters was a nurse in the Lewis Hospital. That was just

Mary (MacFarlane) MacIver, Toronto 1986 (Jim Wilkie)

a couple of years ago, before he died. He died three years ago, and he was 81 when he died.

With the *Metagama,* Murdo MacLean (shipping agent) was going to different schools through the island and showing pictures of out west; of the farmers and the wheat and all that they were growing, and this looked so wonderful. They would come in the evenings and there was a slide show. And there was a Major

# NOTICE

## Exceptional Chance for Lewis Girls
FOR
## Domestic Service in Canada.

MISS YOUNG OF THE COLONIZATION DEPARTMENT OF THE CANADIAN PACIFIC RAILWAY COMPANY, will be at the undermentioned Centres in Lewis for the purpose of interviewing girls who may desire to go to Canada next Spring. The Girls will be accompanied from Stornoway to Montreal and Toronto where they will be placed in situations.

Miss Young who has for many years been connected with this work will give reliable information and guarantee situations.

| | | | |
|---|---|---|---|
| TUESDAY, | 10th December | AIRD PUBLIC SCHOOL, | 6—7 30 p.m |
| „ | „ | BAYBLE | 8 9 30 p.m |
| WEDNESDAY | 11th Dec., | LIONEL | 6 7 30 p.m |
| „ | „ | CROSS | 8—9.30 p.m |
| THURSDAY, | 12th Dec., | CARLOWAY | 7 8.30 p.m |
| „ | „ | SHAWBOST | 9 10 p.m |
| FRIDAY | 13th Dec., | BACK | 7 30 9 p.m |

## HOSTEL TRAINING FOR LEWIS GIRLS AT LENZIE, GLASGOW.

In connection with this Scheme
SUPPORTED BY Mr. T. B. MACAULAY,
Miss Young will receive applications and interview intending applicants.

***All Women interested in this scheme are cordially invited.***

FULL INFORMATION CAN BE OBTAINED FROM

**MURDO MACLEAN,**
46 Point Street, Stornoway.

(Courtesy Glasgow People's Palace)

Goodliff; I had forgotten about him. He went around showing pictures of Calgary and those places.

My brother, Murdo, went out on the *Metagama*. He was the youngest one. The bard went out too, but not until the year after that, and he went to Winnipeg. He had sisters out there . . . I think it was 1924 or '25. His sisters had gone earlier . . . one of them was married and had a house there. I think Annie went out in 1911, and Jessie the following year.

Murdo was only 16 when he went. He was born in 1907 . . . two years older than me. He had just cleared school. I think he was working on the farm with a couple of the Melbost boys. Just the summer before they came they would get a little bit of work to do. Thinning the turnips and that kind of thing, at MacKenzie's Farm – 'Teedy's'. Willie Graham, Murdo MacIver and all that generation. They got a bit of work in the summertime at that farm. All of them came on the *Metagama*. Murdo was the youngest, but there were no restrictions in these days.

The boys were very excited about leaving. I was very homesick after him, when Murdo went. Watching the boat go down the Minch. Everybody in the island was on the pier that day, but if they knew what they were up against, they would never have left home. My brother and another lad, they were supposed to go to a farm in Lindsay, near Toronto. On the train from Montreal they were starved to death. And they used to throw a bag of peanuts into the coaches, you know. Anyway, he got as far as Lindsay at two o'clock in the morning . . . and, nobody to be seen. Nobody to meet him. In the summertime, of course, it was daylight anyway. So it came to five o'clock in the morning and they saw a man coming with a horse and buggy. Anyway, the farmer came and said, 'I suppose I'm the man you're looking for.' And the boys said, 'Yes, I'm sure.' So they went with the farmer, and the other lad didn't stay very long. He worked his way somewhere else. My brother stayed there for three or four months then worked his way up to Fort William – to Thunder Bay – we had an aunt there on my mother's side. He was there working on the grain elevator for a summer, and then he heard that things were brisking up in the States. So he went across there, and that's where he met our relations, the MacKenzie brothers. There were three of them and they got him to go and learn a trade. So he learnt bricklaying in Detroit (1926).

He put in three and a half years and he met a girl from home that he started to go along with and he married her and they settled down in Detroit. Margaret Kennedy, from Calbost, Lochs. She's still in Inverness [Scotland]. They were in Detroit for about four years and the daughter was born, and things were very hard in Detroit then. Everything was flat, so they decided that they would go home. Peggy was only seven months old when they went home, and they settled in Inverness (1932).

I came out in 1927. It was my brother who came out and he sent me my fare. I came to Toronto and the girl he was engaged to, she happened to be home on holiday. I came out with her. I think the fare was £21. That was about it. He thought it was best for me to come here and work here for a little while and then go across to Detroit. I was in service in Stornoway for the Inspector of the Poor, George MacLeod, whose wife was from Melbost, and my aunt knew her. I worked there for maybe a year and a half, or something like that.

When I arrived in Toronto, I came to friends here, and this man who was a great friend of my father, and I had their address. A Lewisman, and his wife was from Tiree, and I stayed with them for two or three days while I went looking for work. The girls could always get work . . . all we knew was housework, anyway! And you had a lovely room to yourself and good food. The wage was only about $40 a month, but, anyway, you had a bathroom to yourself, and the girls didn't do badly here at all. We had every other Sunday off, and a Wednesday afternoon. They didn't have all the convenience that they have today. Instead of going and buying a carton of bleach like they do today, we had to boil the clothes on a two-ring burner, down in the basement. The laundry was really quite a thing to handle.

I was working for a very lovely family . . . in fact, I worked for two families . . . I worked for the head of the provincial police in Toronto, General Williams, him and his wife, and they were very fine people. They were really originally English and they were very kind people, no trouble. Another Canadian girl was working with me, and we did quite well. I got another place with more wages because I was very good at catching on with the cooking and that kind of thing, so I thought – I got the nerve to go into a house and do the cooking. I got married from that house. When I arrived in

Toronto . . . I arrived on a Wednesday. . . and, the following Sunday, I went with this family to the Gaelic Church. And this young man came to me and said, 'Have you relations in Point, in Aird?' And I said, 'Yes, I have, I have a first cousin there.' 'Mary MacLeod?' And I said, 'Yes.' 'Well,' he said, 'you're just her spitting image.' And this is how I met my husband. I never got away from him from that day! [laughs] He was a carpenter (1927).

He came out on the *Metagama*. Norman MacIver from Aird, Point. He went and learned his trade right away. He was farming at home, but he was working with a firm, Milne and Nicholls, and Mr Milne came from Perth, Scotland. They were glad to get anything when they came here first, so he worked as a labourer, but this man, I guess, he could see that my husband was quite intelligent, you know, so he put in his time here and learned his trade in Toronto.

He was in digs with the same people from the time he arrived until the day we were married . . . 20 November 1931. They were Canadian people.

The Gaelic (Free) Church was on Devonport Road and the place was full. There were hundreds of Lewis people here in those days. It was just like being in the island. I used to get homesick once in a while, but I didn't make a fuss about it.

The first job, I did everything in the house . . . laundry, cooking, made beds, looked after children. We had to be on the job at eight o'clock and you were lucky to be through by seven . . . after the supper was over. And you couldn't be out after eleven . . . but it wasn't a bad thing.

The Lewis Society met once a month on a Saturday night. They had it in the Ketchum Hall, right opposite the church on Devonport Road. They had like a concert first, and the dancing after that. Of course, we had to be out before twelve. There were good Gaelic singers here, those days. We used just to get up and sing this and sing that, and sing together. We used to have a cup of tea, and we were the first society in Toronto who started to give you the potatoes and salt herring in the winter time. We made a special night and everybody came from the Caithness Society and the Skye Association . . . and we used to make big money on that!

I hadn't been out of the island before I came here. I hadn't seen a train, I hadn't seen electricity and although there had been a bus from Ness and a bus from Point, I was never in them. I thought,

Free Church, Devonport Road, Toronto (Courtesy *Eilean Nan Fhraoich* magazine)

well, I'm going to pretend as if I know all about this, and that's what I did. I was just working my way carefully, you know, and I noticed how you put the light on and the switch was on the wall . . . and I did the same. Like everyone of us that left the island, I had a lot of learning to do . . . but, never mind, we did very well. If you just make up your mind and be patient, you learn as you go along. It seemed like a very big city, and they were telling me when I arrived at first – Toronto is like a square. If you have the name of the street, you'll always find your way. If your door was not locked at night in those days, you didn't have to worry. Toronto was called 'Toronto the Good', but it's not like that today, of course.

In those days, when young people got married, there were no apartments. You rented a flat from a private family who were buying a home, and you rented the upstairs. You had maybe three rooms, or two rooms, and that's how everybody lived. We were married five years before our son was born, and after he was born, we rented a house for two years. But my husband thought, there's no point in paying rent, let's buy a house . . . so we looked around and, my husband, being a carpenter, we bought an old house for $2,800 in the East End. He turned it inside out and made a beautiful job of it, and we sold it in four years for $6,500. That was our start.

We always stayed in the East End. After a good number of years my husband wanted to build his own house, and he bought a lot in Scarborough. He built it exactly like a house at home, and I'm sure there's not another one in the city like it. It's on Davisville Avenue, and I helped to put the roof on that! He was so proud of that. Then my husband built two houses out at Keswick, away, way out of Toronto, but I didn't like the country. My nerves gave way.

During the depression, we managed. We never had to go on welfare because I went out to work for two and a half dollars a day – they get $45 a day, now, and their car fare – and you could buy a pound of butter those days, for 29 cents. So I kept the wages and, with the bits he was getting in between, we managed fine. But people with four, five or six of a family, they had quite a struggle. Toronto was badly affected.

I went back to Lewis in 1947 for the first time. My husband and I, and Al, who was 12 years old, and we enjoyed it so much. Al spoke Gaelic before he went to school, but after he started school he didn't speak another word.

Lewis wasn't very prosperous when we went back, and we were glad to get back here. Maybe it was the weather – I don't know – but we thought it was a better place to live. But believe me, I wouldn't be here today, only that my roots are here. All my near relations . . . both families . . . are dead. I'm the only one left.

Quite a number of families went home, but my husband felt – we're here, and we have to make the best of it. More stayed [in Canada], of course . . . a lot more. But those who went back, when I spoke to them in 1947, were sorry they ever went over [to Canada]. But what happened . . . those couples had to go into the father's home, or the father-in-law's home. And maybe that don't work so good, sometimes. But those who went back, they said they should have just stayed [in Lewis] and faced it, and they would have been better off. One man we knew, however, thought about coming back to Canada again.

I've had no regrets. The way I was . . . I didn't have parents at home and when I set out my home here I was very happy. And my husband being such a wonderful man . . . it makes a difference. I was very homesick when I came first and now. Lewis is a better place for elderly people to live in. I visited the three homes in Stornoway and I never saw people getting the same attention [in Canada]. Go to a place here . . . the people just break your heart. Canada is a wonderful country for young people, but when you come to a certain age . . . no, no, no.

The developers took the little old church. There's only seven Lewis people there now, and soon there'll be five.

## *Mr and Mrs Angus MacDonald*
## *(Aonghas a' Bhragar)*

*Aird, Tong, Lewis 1987*

*Angus:*

I WAS BORN at 57 South Bragar, in 1903. My father was more of a fisherman, although he also depended on his crops. My mother came from Shawbost. I had six brothers and three sisters, and we went to Bragar school till we were 14.

There were a lot of boats in Bragar at that time, fishing for ling and cod and my father had a fishing boat, but mostly we worked on the croft. It was about 19 miles from Stornoway. I would also get the odd job to do. The houses were the black house type, with thatched roofs.

When I was young I thought about going to the Navy and it was when another fellow and I were in Stornoway to do just that that we heard about the *Metagama*. There was a meeting in Bragar and they showed slides. You know, they showed apples and oranges – but no snowdrifts! Canada was 'the land of sunshine and opportunity', and in a way it was for me. I still get a Canadian pension monthly, and something from the Canadian Navy.

I paid nothing towards my fare at that time. The day the boat sailed, we went over on a bus from Bragar. Two brothers and my stepmother saw me off. It was a sad day. There were eight from Bragar and South Bragar, and five from North Bragar. In one family, the Smiths, there were four brothers . . . two Johns, and two Anguses! There was a special church service in Bragar, and psalm singing on the pier. It really emptied the island of these young men, and if we were overcrowded before we left, they felt lonely after we left!

I don't remember much about the sailing, but I remember going to the Carlsrite Hotel in Toronto for breakfast when we arrived . . . it had been paid for by T. B. MacAulay. I stayed on my farm for three years. It was at Beaverton, Ontario, 70 miles from Toronto, towards Lake Simco. The farmer met myself and another man

Angus and Ishbel MacDonald celebrate their Golden Wedding Anniversary, Tong, 1987 (Courtesy Bill Lucas)

from Bragar, John MacDonald, with a car. Mr MacRae was his name, and the farmers there were keen to have Scots people. The MacRaes were Roman Catholics, but they treated me very well. Some men elsewhere said they were ill-treated.

I was ploughing with horses, and there were sheep, and wheat, oats, hay and corn that they put into silos. I drove four horses with a binder, cutting wheat. I adjusted quite well and the work did my health a lot of good. Also we had good food. I had asthma, but after the three years I was stronger. (Incidentally, my asthma has got better since I came back to Lewis.)

The reason I eventually left the farm was that every autumn you could pay a cheap fare to the prairies and get $5 a day for stooking wheat. This would be 1926. I went out to a place near Calgary, Alberta, and when I came back later that year, I went to General Motors at Oshua, 30 miles from Toronto. I had paid off my $94 to the Government for my fare. I had the receipt until quite recently.

After General Motors I was three seasons on the Lakes. Then the depression came and, in 1932, I went to Thunder Bay. There were camps for men who were building the Trans-Canadian highway, and I was there for three winters. In a way, we really built the country!

I married Ishbel (Thomson, from Tong, Isle of Lewis) in 1937, in Toronto. There was still a bad depression, but I found work in a tannery and we were there for 20 years, apart from five years during the war. For two years, 1947–48, we were back home, and thought of staying, but we went back to Canada, and stayed until 1956. We bought a house in Tong and I worked in the building trade before finishing on the loom. We've been back in Canada two or three times.

When we were in Toronto, I became more active in the Church, and I was converted in 1938. Some who came back, of course, were deported because they hadn't bothered with papers!

*Ishbel:*

I was the sixth child and second girl. My brother, Evander Thomson, went on the *Metagama,* and I went over to Toronto in 1929. I sailed from Glasgow on a similar scheme, run by the Ontario Government, and I worked in domestic service from 1929 to 1937. I first met Angus in the early 'thirties, when he sang at the Toronto Lewis Society Gatherings. I thought he was the proudest man I'd ever seen!

*Angus:*

Maybe I wasn't as proud as herself!

*Ishbel:*

I was supposed to go to a hostel and stayed there at first, but I had a sister and two brothers in Toronto, so I went to stay at my sister's. I worked as a housemaid, waiting at tables, although after we were married I did children's nursing for nine years. We came here in 1956, and we've got one daughter, now in New Zealand.

Funnily enough, I get homesick for Toronto, but I have three brothers and a sister buried in Canada, so it's no wonder my thoughts go back there.

## *Angus MacRitchie*

816 Larchmont Dr.
Daly City
California
November, 1985

I, ANGUS MACRITCHIE, was a passenger on the *Metagama. So* was my younger brother Norman, who passed away in Vancouver a number of years ago.

We went directly to Vancouver and there I married Mary MacDougall from North Uist in 1932. We left Vancouver in 1946 and settled in San Francisco, California, and still live in a suburb, Daly City. We have one daughter and two grandchildren, all living in California, and a number of relatives in Vancouver.

My only brother, Farquhar MacRitchie, LLD, CBE, lives in Aberdeen. He is a retired law professor from Aberdeen University. I wish you luck with the documentary. Hope I'm still around when it comes out. I'm now 84. I was born and brought up in North Dell, Ness.

Yours, etc.,

*Angus MacRitchie*

## *Mary Ann (MacLeod) MacDonald*
### *Tong, Isle of Lewis 1987*

I WAS BORN on this croft in 1900. I had seven sisters and one brother, although one died as a baby. Six of the girls went to America, and I was the fourth. I went to New York in 1921.

My husband, Finlay MacDonald, was from Bayble, in Point, and he came over on the *Metagama*. He came to New York in 1925, but had no visa, and five months later he went to his cousin's in Fort William, Ontario (now Thunder Bay), where he worked on the grain elevators.

I had worked in service in houses on Fifth Avenue and Park Avenue, and latterly I worked with my older sister, who was married. The people we worked for had summer houses in Long Island, Connecticut and New Jersey. They were in real estate, and had enough money not to do anything! Socially we would go to

Mary Anne (MacLeod) MacDonald (left) and sister Murdina (MacLeod) Montgomery (right) (see introduction), Port Washington, 1920s (Courtesy M. A. MacDonald)

Summer house in which Mary Anne worked (Courtesy M. A. MacDonald)

Inside of summer house (Courtesy M. A. MacDonald)

the Lewis or Skye Association dances, and I remember there was a yearly event in Brooklyn.

Anyway, when we got married, we lived in Thunder Bay, and two of our sons, Norman and George, were born there. With the Depression, however, the jobs were gone and my husband's firm, which had its headquarters in Winnipeg, closed without any warning. He went off to work on the Monday and came back after an hour. I said, 'Are you home sick?' The gates had just been locked.

My husband had hopes of getting more work and stayed on for another year, but we came home (1930–31). We took on the Post Office in Tong and then Finlay got a job with the Civil Service in Stornoway. He was an ex-serviceman, and was wounded twice at the Battle of the Somme. He died in 1959.

My oldest sister died in 1986 in America. In the Gaelic tradition, a wake was held in the family home in Lewis.

# *Norman 'Broxy' MacKenzie*

*New York 1986*

My family always lived in Ness and I was born at 32 Habost, August 9th, 1904. My father worked on a croft and then he worked on the mainland, at Kinlochleven Aluminium Works and Rosyth Naval Base. This was before 1910. Then he worked on the [coal] hulks in Stornoway and went where the fishing went . . . Stronsay and places. He broke his leg in 1911 stepping from a drifter to hulk, and hit the gun wheel. I remember the day he came home from hospital. His leg healed but later he was at the Royal Infirmary and they broke it again. And I remember the stitches were from his knee, all the way down.

My mother died when I was ten. There were nine children born into the family, but only two that I remember. The oldest was a boy, Angus, but I only remember Margaret, who was older than me, and Catherine who was younger. Others passed away in infancy . . . a lot of children were dying in those days. There was no medical care and I was fortunate that I didn't attract the measles. It was in Buffalo that I got the measles and the doctor couldn't detect what was wrong with me. He said he never saw anybody that old (27) having measles. In Lewis, a younger brother . . . the doctor came to see him and it had been raining . . . his oilskin was wet. And the child licked his oilskin with thirst. The children in Lewis weren't getting the right care.

I went to Lionel school and I was there till I was 14. I remember the first time I went to Stornoway, in 1916. The carters went over and got a load for the grocery stores and my father was working at the store in Stornoway. He was living in digs, and I took care of the horse and came back the next day. The Stornoway store kept all the merchandise that came from the mainland until the merchants came for it. My father got married again in 1916 and my oldest sister would be away working – at the fishing sometime, gutting. She was in Stronsay when my mother died and was sent for. That's another day I remember . . . when she came home . . . and my mother had been buried.

In my childhood I used to love to go to the shieling. I spent all my summer there. If they could permit me to stay with the cows and bring me food, I wouldn't go home at all! I loved that and I loved the company of the young children. The boys that I was with in those days – one of them came to Canada on the *Metagama* – he was drowned in the Atlantic during the war. Finlay MacDonald. The other boys that were with me in those days went to Australia in 1923. A number of our village boys went there and one was home from New Zealand this summer.

Mostly you had to work on the croft to make a living planting potatoes, or whatever. But I worked for Leverhulme at the Tolsta–Ness road . . . finished school in August 1918 and went to work for Leverhulme in May 1919. Can you guess what I was given [for a wage]? Fourpence an hour! Because I was a nipper. I was getting one pound and four shillings a week and I used to keep the four shillings and give the pound to my father. He was glad to see it.

Just after the war, many of the crofts were looked after by sons, or old people. When the men went to the Navy during the war, the ling and cod fishing died – and never picked up. Same with the herring. I remember my father in those days telling us they used to go to the meetings and Leverhulme was willing to leave Ness alone and even give them the crofts free, and they wouldn't accept because they thought there was a gimmick behind it. I was sorry to see Leverhulme go, but I didn't blame the raiders . . . they were promised land and they should have got it. I thought it was wonderful for those young men that got married and had a family, to get a piece of land where they could build a house for themselves. Being a child then, when Leverhulme came to the island and they used to bring cinematograph shows, showing Port Sunlight, you know, and the work that was going on . . . having no electric, they had to have cinematograph. It was the first movies I ever saw [laughs] and we were, of course, impressed by that.

I'll tell you a story now. I had made an application to come out on the *Metagama*, because the closest friend I had as a young fellow was Finlay MacDonald, and he had made an application. He went back to Lewis during the Depression. I lent him a bit to go to Canada, but I had no money to pay for my landing. My father couldn't give me anything, and we needed four pound ten, for landing. I used to look after the sheep for one of the neighbours

Norman 'Broxy' Mackenzie (left) and friend, Alexander MacFarlane, 1920s (Courtesy N. Mackenzie)

and she promised me that she would give me landing money. When the time came for me to send the money in . . . to fulfil my obligation to the shipping agent . . . I couldn't produce. So I lost out. OK.

It was a big disappointment and that day the *Metagama* left – I cried like anything because I *wasn't* on it! And we came home by car when the *Hebrides* left the quay with the last group. I had just arrived home, having a cup of tea, when she went by the Butt of Lewis and blew, you know? Anyhow, that same day I was over in Stornoway, I applied to the Custom House for RNR (Royal Naval Reserve). We weren't allowed from Ness to go to the RNR – Ness was too far from the Custom House – the Government wouldn't pay for your transportation. So I had an uncle in Point and I gave his address. I was called up in August for a health examination. I went to Chatham and when I came back in the September (1923) all the boys in the village had applied to go to Australia. There were five or six of them, but I had no desire to go to Australia. There was no word of another emigration to Ontario but, fortunately, after that the *Marloch* came out.

I applied to Murdo MacLean, Stornoway, and he wouldn't accept my application because I had reneged on the *Metagama*. So I saw in one of the Highland papers another agent . . . I wrote back, and he accepted my application. But when we were going through the Canadian officials in Lionel school with Murdo MacLean, I remember him telling them, 'This is the person . . .' I don't know if he was saying I had written to the mainland. But anyhow, they accepted me and it was on the SS *Canada* that I got. I was too late for the *Marloch*.

The *Marloch* left on 27 April 1924, and the *Canada* on 17 May 1924. There were quite a few Lewis boys on the *Canada*, but not as many. I was the only one from Habost, but from Lionel there were a number. The deal was the same as the *Metagama*. I went to a farm in Ontario – to Caledonia, fourteen miles from Hamilton. And I worked there for three months. I did everything that I was able to do. Ploughing, milking, cattle. And after three months I decided to leave because I had my fare paid. I was figuring that $120 was paying my fare. [He had received no wages.]

The thought that would come to me was . . . If I go back [to the Ontario Government] they'll punish me for not staying. I believe I was one of the few that remained for a few months. Malcolm MacKenzie had gone with me, but was working in a different place. The first time I went over to see him, he had gone already.

I had a cousin in Buffalo, his name was Angus MacDonald. He's passed away since then, and so has his brother Donald. He sent me $35 while I was on the farm. The farmer didn't know I had it . . . he figured I had nowhere to go. That money kept me going.

The day we arrived in Toronto there were a number of boys who came on the *Metagama* and were working at Niagara Falls. They met us at the train and took us into a restaurant and fed us. I remember I had pork chops! [laughs] These boys, there's one of them still living in Garrabost, Donald MacLean, and he came over to meet his brother. I had no brothers or anybody, but they were

Norman 'Broxy' Mackenzie, 1986 (Jim Wilkie)

friends since schooldays. We were collected by somebody on the train, farmers or immigration people. My farmer's name was Jack Murray. It helped if you'd straighten up, throw back your shoulders and throw out your chest.

As it happened, there were two English boys in the neighbourhood and one of them said to me later, 'I know Jack's difficult to work for.' I'm not saying that he was hard, but if he had even given me $5 a week . . . I couldn't even go to the city. Hamilton was 40 miles away and I didn't even know how to take a bus.

When I left the farm, that's where I went to. There was a Lewisman who became my sister's brother-in-law, and I went to his lodging. He paid his fare, and had a job working in the quarries. Norman Smith. His nickname was 'Power'. I went to his lodging and stayed there a night or two. Then I went to Niagara Falls and, after a few trials, I made it . . . 'illegal'. Somebody went with me who they knew by going back and fore. And I went over and stayed overnight with Donald MacLean. He gave me $2 in the morning and told me to get the high-speed back to Buffalo. The first job I got there, it was one of the boys that came out on the *Metagama,* from Swainbost. John MacLeod. He had been working as a bricklayer/contractor. And I laboured for him and another fellow mixing mortar. When it came to givin' me pay, they had no money, but I went over to see them and it was gettin' close to winter, so one of them gave me an overcoat. A coat was useful to me because I had no clothes . . . the only thing I had was the suit and the winged collar! And overalls to work in.

When I came to Buffalo I was directed to a house where there were Lewis boys, and then there were the boys who came in from the Lakes. There was also a factory nearby, the National Biscuit factory – and there were some boys working there, from Lewis. I worked at the biscuit factory till April 1925 and the Irish foreman told me he wanted me to go to a new plant they were opening in California. But I didn't want to leave all these guys in Buffalo. They started a Lewis Society in Buffalo and I'm sure there would be 200 Lewis people there.

I stayed in Buffalo for six years. I went on the Lakes, again through connections. From Lake Erie you went up to Lake Superior with coal. From Lake Superior you brought iron ore down to Lake Erie. And sometimes you went to Chicago and got a load of grain.

The meeting rooms, 1941 Madison Avenue, Harlem, NYC (Jim Wilkie)

In the winter I got a job in a steel plant. One captain . . . his name was Brown . . . wanted me to go to school for navigation, and I told him all kinds of lies. I couldn't go to Cleveland, being 'illegal'.

I wanted to go to London, Ontario, and apply for a visa. I made application and I had to go to the doctor the first Monday in September, the day after Labour Day (1929). There were no trains running in Ontario then, so I got somebody in Buffalo to drive me over to Southampton, and as he passed the doctor's address, he was standing on the verandah. He saw me coming out of the car, and made me nervous. He said, who was I with, with a New York licence plate? And I certainly didn't tell him the truth, but he shouldn't have had anything to do with that. He says, 'You workin' on a farm? Show me your hands. I don't see any callouses.' So he wouldn't let me through.

At the beginning of 1930 they opened the quota for British subjects and I went over to Hamilton with another fellow and tried again. He got through. I didn't. Well, my life was ruined as far as Buffalo was concerned.

'Where were you born?' was always the first question. 'Where are you working? How long are you going to stay over?' Then, I didn't care what would happen because I was desperate. Once, I didn't tell an immigration man a word of truth except that I was born in Scotland. He says. 'I believe everything you say, except that you were born in Scotland. You've got the map of Ireland all over you!' You see what we went through?

Well, I had a cousin in New York who was also 'illegal', so I came down and went to work in the tunnel, the next day or the next night and there were, oh, lots of Lewismen. None of them were married. This was the water tunnel, 1930. Annie [wife, also from Lewis] arrived on 1 April 1930, and I came to New York on the 3rd. I worked in the tunnel for a year and a half, and the job was finished.

The Depression was really on, but I got a job as an apprentice house painter, at $2 a day. And I worked for 35 years, for four different companies, painting. The last company painted the Radio City Complex.

We got married in 1937 and our children were born in 1937 and 1943. I heard from someone that there was a British contract so I went over to the British consul and told them I was illegal. I was sent to 42nd Street, then the main New York Post Office on 8th Avenue. One of them thought that having been on the Lakes I was OK, but asked, 'Why didn't you do this before?' I said I didn't know I could do anything. I was afraid of men in uniform coming after me. So, I made an application – 23 pages in triplicate – of everywhere I'd been since I was 18. They took my fingerprints and sent them to Buffalo. They wrote back saying there was nothing against me.

I wrote to Ness, but didn't get a report back. Finally, something came from Dingwall, but meanwhile the American emigration wrote to say, 'Forget about it.' I was legal.

In the 'thirties, the Lewis Society was going on up in Harlem. At eight o'clock on a Saturday night – nobody bothered you – the girls who worked as domestics would go up there to the hall. There were four Scottish societies met in that hall – Lewis, Lewis and Skye, the Celtic Society and the New York Gaelic Society – and they all got together on a Saturday night. Maybe 400 Scottish people in New York, congregating in Harlem, for a dance.

They had religious meetings there, too. We used to get ministers from the Free Church, on their way to Detroit. And the owners of the hall were getting so much off (rates) because there were religious services in the buildings.

# *Murdo M. MacLean*

*Montreal 1986*

I WAS BORN in Habost in January 1908. I come off a very long-lived bunch of people from Ness. I have a genealogical table that goes back to the seventeenth century and there's nobody who's not a Niseach.

I went to Lionel primary school and we had very good teachers. We were well grounded in the basics and when I went to High School at the Nicolson, I had read just about all the classics. They took a very dim view of us using Gaelic and we didn't start 'learning' it (as an academic subject) until we went to Nicolson. I had excellent Gaelic teachers, James Thomson, especially.

I was never in Stornoway until I left to go to the Nicolson. There were no cars. They were just beginning to get beaten-up, second-hand old buses on the road. And it was expensive to go there. The traditional way of going was a horse and cart, and it was a day's journey from Ness. There wasn't a bit of paved road in rural Lewis . . . it was all gravel.

I was a self-motivated sort of student, but when I was 16 I chucked the Nicolson. It was the boarding and the boredom. [laughs] I worked on the croft for a couple of years – that was an education in itself. My father was getting on in years and my brother was working in a shipyard in Glasgow. Somebody had to do the work. So I stooged around till I was 18, then, in desperation, I joined the regular army.

My father was a stonemason and he always had little projects going. They were beginning to put up white houses then. And he used to come to the shieling – which was halfway between Tolsta and Ness – for the weekends. He was the one who renewed the stonework in the ancient temple at Europie, in 1912, when the Anglican Church decided to re-roof it. He also worked on the restoration at Fort Augustus. As a matter of fact, when I was a kid, they used to call me 'Mac Fort Augustus'! To be a young boy in Lewis was paradise!

Leverhulme was down in Port of Ness a lot and I used to follow him around like a little dog, with all the other kids. When they started building the Ness–Tolsta road, everybody in Ness had a paypacket. Ordinarily, to get a paypacket you had to leave the island, go to Glasgow . . . someplace where the work was.

But I wouldn't want to see the island industrialised . . . belching smoke and factory whistles blowing at six o'clock in the morning. If they wanted that they could go south for it, and that's what they told him. At the meetings, somebody would get up . . . and they didn't lack for people who would defend their position very fluently. If there's one thing about a Lewisman, he's full o' words, if nothing else! [laughs] There was a tremendous thirst for land. If you didn't have a piece of land, you were nothing.

The [older] boys were not redundant . . . they wanted out. There was no way you could have contained me in that island, no matter what you offered me – but the taking away of the young people was also a disaster, because it left those without strength behind. I wanted to see everything and experience everything. And there were a lot like that. Quite a number of the people who sailed on the *Metagama* would have been war veterans, but they were no sooner back than they [the Government] were talking about getting rid of them . . . because they were an incubus . . . they didn't know what to do with them. I think the wanderlust is always there, though. I think it is a Celtic trait.

The [*Metagama*] day started off early and I swear, as a young boy of 16, I remember it just like it was yesterday. Most of the population of Lewis were in Stornoway that day, and I remember two things that made the situation worse than it was – if that's possible. The Gaelic psalms – if you're a Gaelic speaker, it gets you right here in your heart – and the band marching up and down. It was really pathetic to see these people embarking on that boat . . . and the mothers crying, 'We're never going to see you again.' And, you know, 90 per cent of them were right.

She sailed up the Minch, and there's a place there called St Ronan's Temple – a little green hill, a mile or so from the lighthouse at the Butt. The people of Europie made a big, big bonfire and, just as the sun was going down, the *Metagama* went around there and the fire was the last thing they saw at sunset. And I remember somebody telling me years and years later, a Ness boy, that it was

Murdo M. MacLean, Montreal, 1986 (Jim Wilkie)

just touch and go for him jumping overboard, two or three miles off the Butt. And he said many's a time since then he wished he had. He was one of those people who were chronically homesick.

I had quite a few relatives on board – two uncles, one of whom had been in Canada before, and the two of them got work in Scotstoun, Quebec, in the easter townships from a man who owned a sawmill and who was my grandfather's brother. He had gone out, way back, and everyone that came there from Lewis got a job.

Some years, I came into Stornoway to attend a concert at the Town Hall, and T. B. MacAulay was the guest of honour. I was walking along Cromwell Street and on the other side, just about where the parking lot is, Johnny Gray [teacher] was walking along the other side towards me. He saw me and took the trouble of crossing the street. And he said, 'MacLean, where have you been since you left school?' I said, I've been in the army.' He says, 'You bloody fool.' He was principal of the school when Gibson left, in the 'twenties. He says, 'I got a proposition for you. My graduating class are sitting the MacAulay/Sun Life examination tonight up at the school and those who pass will be offered employment in Montreal.' I said, 'That sounds very interesting, but I don't suppose

I've got a cat in hell's chance of passing.' He says, 'Of course you have.'

So I was going along and thinking this over when I met an old pal of mine from South Dell. He was working in a garage in Stornoway and he says, 'Let's go and have a pint or two.' Well, we went and had a pint or two . . . and a pint or two. He was living in a boarding house in Plantation Road, and I woke up in the morning . . . asleep on the floor. 'Well,' I said, 'I didn't half blow a chance last night.' I had a big, fat head, but I thought of this and I thought of it. Finally, I made my way up to the school, and Johnny Gray was in his office. He said, 'What happened?' and I said, 'I got sidetracked.' 'Well,' he said, 'Mr Duckworth is coming in this morning to check the results . . . maybe he'll allow you to take the test by yourself.'

So Duckworth came in, agreed, and they put me up in Room 2A with the exam paper and a whole flock of blank paper. At the required time, Johnny Gray came and collected the paper. I walked up and down, wondering what was my fate. After Duckworth had looked it over, Gray came bounding up the stair and, as I was passing through the open door, he patted me on the back. [laughs] When I got to MacRae's office, Duckworth's standing there with his raincoat on and his hat in his hand. He stuck out his hand and sald, 'When do you want to sail?'

This was June (1929) and I told him I wanted to finish the croft work because I had an invalid father and there was nobody else to do the work. Would it be alright if I deferred until September? He says OK. Go and see Murdo MacLean [shipping agent] and we'll have somebody meet you when you get off the boat.

I sailed from Liverpool on the *Duchess of Atholl* – 20 September 1929. I went into the mathematical division at Sun Life, and we were the actuaries, working on mortality tables and all kinds of statistics for agents. I finished up a supervisor of that department with a staff of 45 and I met my wife (also from Lewis) in the investment library at Sun Life. She passed an exam too.

When I came out, day after day in September – nothing but blue skies and sunshine. They put me in a hotel for three days until they found me a place to stay. I finished up with two Glasgow ladies, a block from the office. Talk about landing on my feet! And when I told my brother I was earning $125 a month (£25) he couldn't believe it. He was earning £3 a week and came home looking as though he'd been crawling up a sewer! He lived in Govan. By the time I was here three months I said, 'This great, big, beautiful country is mine!'

The day we were supposed to leave . . . from Glasgow . . . it was the time of the equinoxial gales and there was a terrible storm raging. So the boat couldn't leave. We had to go to Liverpool Harbour and they sent us by train, from Glasgow. Even the next day she [the boat] got bashed against the dockside and damaged, but not enough to deter her from leaving. Then across to Belfast to take on some people and away. With me in the cabin were three other people headed for Sun Life, and I remember one incident which reflects more or less the way we felt. The steward came through the lounge and said 'Last sight of land, ten minutes.' So we went out, holding on to the rail. I remember us holding out our glasses and looking at the last light and saying, 'Goodbye, and thanks for nothing!'

I had done everything to get a job in Dover when I got my discharge. The only two offers were prison guard, or coal mining. So I came home very bitter, and I left the British Isles very bitter. But we were starting out with a clean sheet and it finally dawned on me that I had what it took to make it there after about six months.

We had a Lewis Society in Montreal. We rented a hall on Saturday nights and had a ceilidh. But when the day comes when I'm alone, I'm going home. For at least six months a year. Here I am, almost 80 years old – and I'm making plans!

# *Lloyd Leland*

*Moncton, New Brunswick 1986*

I WAS BORN in October 1917, in a little woodland community in Penfield, New Brunswick, where nobody lives now. There was a total of four families and we lived by farming and fishing. I only lived there for the first few years of my life.

My father and mother were both born in New Brunswick, my father in Mascarene and my mother in Caithness. Both places had been settled originally by Highland settlers, mostly from Sutherlandshire and Perthshire. Mother was a MacLeod whose people came over in 1804 . . . her great grandparents came from a place 26 miles east of Cape Wrath. That place probably doesn't exist now either!

They had psalm books and bibles, so they probably read and wrote Gaelic. Their children spoke it, their grandchildren understood it, then that was the end of it. My mother's father would have understood Gaelic and the last Gaelic speaker in our community was Dan Matheson, who lived up the road from us. He died in 1945, aged 99. By then we were in the parish of St George, 15 miles from Penfield. Wooden houses, of course, and the house we moved to is still standing.

I also remember a house that belonged to my grandfather's father. The house was torn apart and rebuilt in another place. I was around seven and I remember finding the old Gaelic Bible. Even at that age I had the feeling that that was my old culture, and I remember that 1923 was what they called 'The Year of the Freshet'. A freshet is a spring flood, and the floods were particularly bad in New Brunswick that spring.

St George parish was small farming, fishing and cutting wood in the wintertime. Pulp wood and lumber. Otherwise, not unlike crofting. A few people used two horses, but more often there was one horse. My father was one of the last people to use oxen in our area – although I don't remember them. St George would be about 50 miles from St John, by road.

Everybody was a carpenter, mason, whatever had to be done. They built 'weirs' in the sea to catch the herring. You put these big logs – pilings – down. Some of them might be 50 feet long. You drive them in a big circle and they put racks in between them woven of smaller staff they called brush. And then, on top of that they had the top nest where they strung netting on. You see, we have these big tides here, 28 feet, sea tides. In some years the herring would be good. It was done all along the sea coast, the rivers and estuaries. Every thousand feet along the shore there were 'weir privileges'. You paid the Government for a licence. Generally speaking, there were no such things as landlords. Someone might rent a place, but it was very unusual.

I started school in September 1924. I would be seven years old. All the kids were country children of Scots descent. No French or any other nationalities. As boys, there weren't enough of us to have hockey teams. We would play on the ice and maybe chase a frozen lump around with a hockey stick. Of course, we had a lot of work to do. In those days, before electricity – washing machines, churns, and grindstones for sharpening axes operated by boy-power! But it was good for us in a way. Since I've been married 41 years ago my wife has seen me off work two weeks, when I had mumps! [laughs] Our staple diet was the same as Highlanders – fish and potatoes!

We didn't feel remote because we had contact with people in the cities – although we felt a little different from these people, from Boston, and so forth. The first time I saw a train we were out blueberrying in Penfield and I was off by myself when this thing came along. I suppose it was travelling around 25 mph. It was the most tremendously impressive, and fastest thing I'd ever seen. A steam engine.

The nearest neighbour would be about 100 yards away, the next nearest about half a mile away. You could go outdoors and shout, and nobody would hear you. [laughs] We went to church on Sunday . . . the local church we went to was called the Baptist Church, and there was also a Campbellite Church down the road. Campbellites call themselves Disciples of Christ, now, similar to Baptists, with communion every Sunday. They had been formed by some man named Campbell in the US who was a Presbyterian, but reformed into a type of Baptist. They believed in adult baptism and communion every Sunday. Sometimes, in the 'twenties, after

Lloyd and Cathy Leland, Moncton, New Brunswick, 1986

church, you'd meet a Gaelic speaker, a stranger who was maybe over from Prince Edward Island, or somewhere. Nobody from the Old Country.

There were people better off than we were, and people worse off. I think my mother made a good manager. [laughs] My mother lived to be 90 and could cut and split wood along with the best of them. She would look after cows and sell butter in town. And she had hens that laid all winter long – when eggs fetched a good price, because nobody else's were laying. She knew that it didn't matter about hens being cold, but they had to be dry. She let them have lots of ventilation and fed them curd from skimmed milk, and things like this. I still feel like a country boy.

During the Depression, the people worked in the woods. If they got any sale for their pulp, the best they could get was maybe $6 a cord (136 cubic feet of wood). A lot of work when you cut it with an axe. It would go to the pulp mill for making paper and the $6 was for the man who owned the land. The worker only got two dollars a cord and you worked from seven in the morning till seven at night. And I also dug for clams (not scallops) in the mud, for 80 cents a barrel.

We didn't have any direct contact with Indians, although we used to see them. They'd maybe come over to St George to play baseball. Sometimes they'd come round selling baskets too. There was what we called a Reserve on the American side, but those Indians actually belonged in our territory, and there was a tradition that the Indian had a right to take a tree that he needed, like an ash tree, from anybody's land. We believed that the Indian had a right to hunt all the year round if he so desired, but they've been pushed back and back. One Indian friend says, 'You didn't have to tell the Indian about a hunting season. We knew when animals were having their young, and things like this.' I think the Indians have been very much wronged and they live very badly now, like low-class white people . . . too much paternalism, protectionism and, you might say, socialism. I think you have to protect the weak who can't look after themselves, but you can go overboard with this.

I went to California in 1938 and took a course in aircraft maintenance. I went to school up there, subsidised by my father to a certain extent, and I subsidised myself by working. I was in Glendale, a suburb of Los Angeles.

The first contemporary Gael I met, I was visiting my brother in Baltimore, when I was in the air force, during the war. He brought a couple of fellows from a ship that was next to his shop into a pub, and we spent the evening there. They were Lewis boys, three of them actually. Later, of course, I married a Leosach (Cathy, from Point).

## *Note*

1. Lloyd Leland has spent most of his working life in the aircraft industry, but is also a gifted linguist and he and his wife use Gaelic as their everyday language.

# *James R. Macleod*

323 Broad Street
Lake Geneva
Wisconsin USA
53147
7/2/86

Dear Mr Wilkie,

I am in receipt of your recent letter relating to my departure from Lewis on that memorable day. First of all let me say that I cannot guarantee that I will be here on any particular occasion that would seem favourable to you, as I do go places. But I will endeavour to recall as much as I can possibly do concerning my departure from Lewis and any subsequent experiences up until now and forward them on to you.

However, could you possibly help a lot by writing me with questions concerning it all? Will be looking forward to hearing from you.

Sincerely,

*James R. MacLeod*

James R. MacLeod, photographed with his sisiter

Page 2, March 20, 1986, Regional News, Lake Geneva, WI

# MacLeod Service Held

Rev. James R. MacLeod, 89, died Friday, March 14, of an apparent heart attack at his residence in the Metropolitan Church Association headquarters, 323 Broad Street. He had returned home two days earlier from Lakeland Hospital where he had been treated for flu and other complications.

He was born Jan. 8, 1897, in the Town of Ness on the Isle of Lewis, Scotland, the son of Norman and Annie Banks MacLeod. During World War I, he served with the British Army in France. As a young man he came to Canada and from there to Detroit, MI. On a street corner in Detroit, he heard Metropolitan Church people proclaiming the gospel and decided to join their organization.

MacLeod entered the Metropolitan Bible School in Waukesha in 1925 where he took Bible training and also was the school's cook and shoe repairman. He married Alma Clark in Detroit in 1943 and they had one daughter who died in infancy.

MacLeod was pastor of Metropolitan churches in Detroit; Toronto; Dunbar, PA and in Maine. MacLeod was remembered throughout his pastoring area and in Lake Geneva by his distinct Scotch brogue.

In 1970, MacLeod and his wife moved to Lake Geneva from Dundee, IL and he did administrative work at the association headquarters. They then moved to Florida where his wife died in 1976, after which he returned to Lake Geneva.

MacLeod is survived by a sister, Miss Catherine MacLeod, Isle of Lewis, Scotland.

Final rites were held at 2:30 PM Sunday at the Steinke Funeral Home. Rev. Warren W. Bitzer, head of the Metropolitan Church Association, officiated. Burial was in Prairie Home Cemetery, Waukesha.

# *Hugh Fraser*

Burnaby
British Columbia
Canada
12th April, 1984

I WAS BORN in Stornoway on 7 June 1902, but raised in Gravir, Park. I finished grade seven in school and, in 1917, with two other Gravir boys, went to Glasgow to serve an apprenticeship with the intention of becoming a marine engineer. The other two boys, John Murdo and Donald Angus Matheson, who were cousins, apprenticed as ship's carpenters. We all got started at Messrs Stephens, Linthouse.

I took up boxing as a sports sideline, winning the industrial championship at my weight throughout the city. I also won the Cadet, the Brigade and the Territorial championships. In 1922 I took part in the West of Scotland boxing championships, winning the 9st 9lb class, and won it again in 1923. Shortly after this I was laid off at work, with hundreds of others. The war being over, shipbuilding came to an end, and unemployment became the rule of the day.

I made my way home to Gravir, and was there until I sailed from Stornoway with many other young Lewis people for Canada, aboard the SS *Marloch,* on Saturday April 26, 1924. We had lovely weather, and smooth sailing all the way until we reached Quebec city, late Saturday. We disembarked on Monday morning, May 5th, and received our landing cards, which I have still in my possession. With many others, I headed for Toronto, Ontario, and was met by some who came to Canada in 1923. Conditions didn't look good, unemployment was high.

I happened to get a job with a number of Stornoway boys, with Willy's Overland Export Department. The company had received an order from France for cars, which had to be dismantled and boxed for shipping. Then in Sept '24 a harvest excursion was initiated, resulting in a great manpower move westward, the fare being so cheap. I went harvesting (stooking and thrashing) barley, oats and wheat, at a place 200 miles west of Winnipeg, Manitoba, after which I went to Winnipeg.

In 1925, on New Year's Day, I competed in a boxing tournament and won the welterweight (10st 7lb) class championship of Manitoba, and won it again in 1926. In 1926 I was chosen to represent Manitoba with three other boxers and two wrestlers in the Dominion Boxing and Wrestling Championships, held at New Westminster, BC. I won my way into the finals of the Middleweight (11st 6lb) class, but damaged my hand in the event. I was thus badly handicapped and lost on points when I boxed at my natural (welter) weight. I didn't compete in the middleweight finals.

One of the wrestlers and myself stayed at Vancouver where I started boxing professional after my hand healed. Although the stakes in those days weren't high, it was enough to keep the wolf of want from the door. In the summer of '26, a friend, Angus MacLean, and I headed for the interior of BC where we got a job with the Consolidated Mining and Smelting Company of Canada.

I worked as a mechanic at the Concentrator for three years, during which time I won the professional welterweight championship of Western Canada. My last boxing engagement was on November 30th 1929, for fifteen days later I walked into an old garage that had been converted into a Full Gospel Hall and surrendered my life to the Lord. On Monday evening after work I went to see my trainer and manager, and told him, to his great disappointment, what had happened, and that I couldn't beat up my fellow men anymore.

After my decision, I felt a great urge to learn how to study the Bible and aquaint myself with God's will for my life. In September 1930 I decided to go to a Bible College and take a two-year course, after which I intended to return to my job in Kimberley. During my two years in Bible College the great Depression set in, and I think it was at this time many returned back to Britain.

I returned to Kimberley and stayed with my brother-in-law for a while. Eventually I got a call to do some Gospel ministry which I ventured on tremblingly, being more or less a pioneer work.

In 1934 I met the girl who, a few months later, became my very precious wife. She was a deaconness. We got married in Edmonton, Alberta, in her home church. After this we continued ministering in various towns in BC, Alberta and Saskatchewan, until 1941.

The war by this time had drained much of Canada's manpower and a general appeal went out for tradesmen to work in shipyards and other industries. My folks at home in Gravir also needed financial help. After much prayer and consultation with our general superintendent, I went to work as an engine fitter in a Vancouver shipyard, until the end of the war, after which I went to sea as an engineer. On my first trip I was able to get four days off the ship to go to Glasgow and meet my precious brother for the first time in 24 years.

In January 1948 I got a job as stationary chief engineer with a multi-million dollar wholesale food, merchandise and vegetable establishment, where I continued employment until April 1973. The company retired me at 71, six years beyond retirement age. We have two sons and one daughter.

Your sincerely,

In the bonds of Calvary,
*Hugh Fraser*

*(Letter to Norman Malcolm MacDonald)*

# *John MacDonald – Seonaidh Shiurra*

*Fivepenny, Isle of Lewis*
*Comunn Eachdraidh Nis 1980*

'S E BLIADHNA air fhichead a bha mise nuair a dh'fhalbh mi air a' *Mhetagama*. Dh'fhalbh mise seach nach robh cail ann an seo a dheanadh mi – cha robh cail ann a seo. Sin man a dh'fhalbh a h-uile duine againn. Dh'fheumadh tu falbh taobh-eigin airson do bhithbeo. Bha representative bho Ontario, Canada, ann an seo as a sgoil 's air feadh an eilein gu leir 's faodaidh tu bhi cinnteach gu robh e toirt gealltanas math seachad. Co dhiubh, dh'fhalbh da dhuine dheug againn bho'n taobh thall – 's e sin an Cnoc Ard, na Cóig Peighinnean 's Eoropaidh. Well, 's e dithis eile 's mi fhein a tha beo dhiubh. Tha seasar de bhalaich an taobh thall air an tiodhlaiceadh ann a Buffalo.

'S ann a Steornabhagh a dh'fhalbh sinn air a' *Mhetagama* agus 's e April a bh'ann, deireadh April, 's bha duil gur ann a Montreal a bha i dol a landadh. Cha b'ann, chan fhaight' ann aig an deigh – bha na icebergs arm an sin agus 's ann a St John, New Brunswick – 's ann a landaig sinn. Bha cuisean gle thruagh air a' *Mhetagama* fhein – cha robh cail ann ach three square meals. Sud far na dh'fhairich mise cheud acras ceart. o, bha torr dhaoine innt'. Sgap iad – chaidh sinn suas a Thoronto a h-uile duine bh'ann 's sgap iad air falbh a sin.

Chaidh mise agus Domhnull Chrut a bh'aig an tigh annan seo bho chionn da bhliadhna, chaidh sinn gu tuathanaich a mach, ach cha b'ann gu'n aon thuathanach a chaidh sinn. Agus cha robh moran de obair aige aig an am ud ann, bha e an deidh 's am barr a chur sios, an talamh a threabhadh agus a h-uile cail ach cha do dh'fhuirich sinne ach coig latha an deidh sin. Bha sinn faisg air a cheile. Thainig sinn a sin a steach a Thoronto a rithis an ceann an coig neo sia laithean. Chaldh sinn dhan an Employment Exchange arm an sin. Chuir iad sios sinn gu Niagara Falls – shios Niagara River. Thug sinn ann an sin fad an t-samhraidh. Bha e gle mhath 'g obair aig Hydro Electric Scheme (Hydro Electric Power Commission of Ontario). Cha robh am pàigheadh dona idir

John MacDonald (Seonaidh Shiurra), Fivepenny, Isle of Lewis (Courtesy Comunn Eachdraidh Nis)

's bha sinn a'fuireach ann an camp. Agus b'e an camp e, cha robh sinne ann am boarding-house a riamh dha leithid cho math. Bha na h-eolaich comhla ri cheile man a bha sinn ann an seo fhein – chan eil mi gle chinnteach mu dheidhinn cianalas, bha's comhla ri cheile. The culmhn' agam air bonfire a bhi 'ga fhaicinn bho'n a' *Mhetagama* nuair a bha sinn ri dol tarsuinn arm an seo.

Bha am pàigheadh gu math ach bha agad ri obrachadh – gu h-araid arms na States – bha obair chruaidh ann. Chaidh sinn a null gu Detroit bho na Niagara Falls nuair a sguir sinn ann. O, fhuair sinn obair shios aig a'phower house, Bha sinn an latha seo air an t-sraid – dh'fhag sinn an joba sin co dhiubh – 's ann a thuirt mo nabuidh, Domhnull, rium, 'Eil thu ag aithneachadh an duine sin air taobh thall na sraid?' 'Chan eil,' ars mise. Bha esain ri gaireachdainn – Domhnull. 'Well,' ars esain, 'tha mise smaoineachadh gur e Alasdair MacThomais a th'ann.' 'S e sin Alasdair Ruadh na Criadhaidh. Co dhiubh, ann an ceann greis thainig e nall – chan fhaca mise an dulne riamh. Sheall mise ris mus d' thainig e nall 's thuirt mi, 'Well, ga 's bi co th'ann, 's e Gaidheal a th'ann co dhlubh.' Thainig e nall's dh'aithnicheadh Domhnull e – bha Domhnull ag obair le caraichean Dhomhnuill Iain Oig ann an seo 's bhiodh iad ri dol thuige leis na messages agus an ceann greis thainig e nall. 'An tu a th'ann, a Dhomhnuill?' ars esain. 'O, 's e,' arsa Domhnull, 'bha mi smaoineachadh gu robh mi 'gad aithneachainn.' 'Co as a tha fear tha comhla riut?' ars esain. 'Tha a Eoropaidh,' ars Domhnull. 'Co leis e?' o, dh'inns Domhnull. 'O, feir, a bhalaich, mo chairdean,' ars esain.

Bha e worraigeadh airson joba agus 'Fhalbh 's seall ris an uinneag a tha thall an sin a bheil cail arm a ghabhas tu,' arsa Domhnull ris. Agus dh'fhalbh e null. Thuirt mise ri Domhnull, 'Tha'n duine ud a'worraigeadh airson joba – gheibh e jobannan gu leor a seo.' Bha aon ait' ann co dhiubh, dh'aithneachadh sinn fhein balaich a bha 'g obair arm. Bha iad ag inns dhuinn gu robh an obair cruaidh. Ach chuirear Alasdair – chaidh sinn a mach gu Fisher building ann an East Detroit dh'fhalbh sinn leis. Bha tri queuechean ann an sin shift a'tighinn a mach 's shift a'dol a steach, third shift ri dol a dh'iarraidh am pàigheadh chun an oifis agus thuirt sinn ri Alasdair, 'Fhalbh dhan a qhueue sin chun an oifis.' Dh'fhalbh Alasdair dhan a qhueue's cha robh e fada gun a thighinn le cairt mhor ghorm aige. 'Bhalachaibh,' ars esain, 'tha mi startadh right away air an shift oidhche.' 'O, gle mhath,' ars sinne. Thuirt e gum bu choir dhuinn fhein a dhol as deidh job arm cuideachd ach bha fios againn gur e obair uamhasach cruaidh a bh'ann.

Thuirt sinn ris gun coinnicheadh sinn e a leithid seo a dh'oidhche anns a leithid seo a dh'ait' – oidhche Shathuirn. Fhuair sinn fios gu Walter 'an Mhurchaidh – bha e ann an Detroit an uairsin – gu robh Alasdair anns a'bhaile 's choinnichear Alasdair ann an sin shios. Ma dh'fhag sinne gaireachdainn, dh'fhag Walter. Chaidh foighneachd de dh' Alasdair de man a bha an jobs cordadh ris.

'O, cha do rinneadh a'bhruid fhein airson da uair dheug a thide 'san oidhch',' ars esain. 'Chan eil am paidhir mheatag a'seasamh ach aon uair a thide dhomh.' Cha robh moran ri fhaicinn ann an Alasdair ach gu dearbha bha e cruaidh. Dh'fhuirich e ann an sin air an shift oidhche airson coig miosan. Chaidh e an uairsin suas gu Chicago – chaidh e air dredge ann an sin 's cha do charaich e riamh dhith gus an tainig e dhachaidh arm an seo.

Ach 'sann gu na Lakes a chaidh mise an uairsin – air soithichean, steamairean a'tarraing gual 's gron – iron ore – a nuas bho Lake Michigan 's bho Lake Superior. Thug mise ann an sin gus an tainig mi dhachaidh ann a seo. Bha'n obair a'cordadh riunn gun teagamh 's bha'm pàigheadh ann na b'fhearr na dheanadh duine ann an àit sam bith eile dhan duthaich.

Bha society againn ann an sud ann am Buffalo. Bha fear elle againn ann an Cleveland–Lewis Society – bha e ann an Detroit cuideachd. Cha mhor nach robh arms a h-uile baile a sud 's bhiodh sinn a'coinneachadh uair 'san t-seachduinn. Man a biodh ceilidh ann, bhiodh partaidh neo rudeigin. Bha e cuideachdail gu leor, h-abair sin.

Ach ged a bham pàigeadh gu math, bha'n obair cruaidh. Bhiodh sinn ag obair uairean torr nas fhaide ne anns duthaich seo. Cha robh obair Sabaid ann an ait' – chan fhaca mis' ait' anns an robh obair Sabaid. Cha do ghabh mis' aithreachas falbh as a seo idir – cha robh rum aithreachas agad – cho fada's a bha an t-slaint' againn. Bha am biadh gu math anns a h-uile aite cuideachd – biadh math. Thug mise thall naoi neo deich bliadhnaichean. Chan eil moran a dh'fhalb air a' *Mhetagama* beo. Tha Domhnull MacLeoid beo – Domhnull Tullag as a'Chnoc Ard, Aonghas Domhnullach a Eoropaidh – Aonghas Iain Dhudhaill, agus Calum MacLeoid – Calum na Leadaidh.

## *Donald 'Chrut' MacLeod*

*Buffalo*

*Comunn Eachdraidh Nis 1980*

'S E FICHEAD bliadhna bha mis nuair a dh'fhalbh mi air a' *Mhetagama* ann an April 1923. Cha robh obair ann an seo ann, cha robh thu deanamh cail ach'na do sheasamh ris na cruachan. Cha robh cail ann – tide an aitich 's na monach bhiodh tu ag obair an uairsin, ach nuair a thogadh tu am buntata's t-fhoghar cha robh thu deanamh cail.

Thainig am fear seo, Major Goodlive, dha na sgoilean 's theann e ag innse dhuinn an opportunity a bh'ann an Ontario's gum biodh joba againn aig an tuathanach nuair a ruigeadh sinn sin. 'S dh'fhalbh sinn a Steornabhagh – thug driftear sinn a mach chun a' *Mhetagama* – bha i inuigh as a' Bhay. Chaidh sinn air bord – timchioll air tri cheud againn na tri cheud gu leth.

Agus bha Steornabhagh lan an oidhche mas do dh'fhalbh sinn, cha robh uiread ann a riamh 's a bh'ann an oidhche ud. Chan fhaigheadh tu sios an t-sraid, bha na ceudan dhaoine ann an oidhch' ud. Chan eil cail a dh'fhios agams cait na chaidil iad. Arms a'mhadainn chaidh sinn troimh 'n an stor a bha sud 's bha doctairean an sin 's bha iad 'gad examinigeadh mas deach sinn sios dhan driftear's thug an driftear a mach chun a' *Mhetagama* sinn. 'S bha ministearan ann an sin – tha cuimhn' agam gu robh an da mhinistear a Nis arm co dhiubh. Bha iadsan ag urnuigh mas do dh'fhalbh sinn. 'S chaidh iadsan air ais agus sheol sinn. Dol a null man a Rudha chaidh balach a mhuinntir Chrois a bha thall ann an Canada roimhe sin, chaidh esain suas agus dh'fhoighnich e dhan sgiobair, would he blow three blows on the whistle going by the Butt, and he did. Och, cha robh an trup dona idir a'dol a null.

Bha a h-uile duine og 's cha robh fios gu de bha thall an sud – miann-achadh gum biodh tu ann ann an latha no dha gus a faiceadh tu de seorsa tir a bh'ann. Bha latha neo dha againn a bha fladhaich – bha torr le cur-na-mara orra, Bha chlann-nighean tinn airson tri neo cheithir a laithean. Bha sinn a'dol suas gu Montreal ach nuair a rainig sinn sin chan fhaigheadh sinn suas, bha deighean ann, 's chaidh sinn sios gu St Johns, New Brunswick – thug sinn da latha dheug dol a null. Thainig mise null bho chionn tri seachduinnean ann a sia uairean a thide. Och, bha sinn a'faighinn biadh gu leor – tri bidh a h-uile latha. Cha robh thu faighinn torr.

Co dhiubh, rainig sinn St Johns – chaidh sinn chun an treine, 's ann a bha 'wash-out' air a 'rail-road'. Chan fhaigheadh sinn air adhart gu Montreal. B'fheudar dhuinn fuireach ann an sin airson latha. Bha'm biadh air an treine air fas gann 's chuir iad air bord, a 'sister ship' a' *Mhetagama* sinn – bha ise a St Johns. Fhuair sinn bladh math a sin.

Nuair a charaich iad a 'rail-road', chaidh sinn air an treine rithis 's dh'fhalbh sinn gu Toronto. Rainig sinn Toronto 's chaidh sinn a steach gu bracoisd dha hotel an sin – a h-uile duine againn. Dol suas eadar St Johns agus Toronto fhuair a h-uile duine joba airson a dhol chun an tuathanaich. Bhiodh tu faighinn ticard bho Major Goodlive le ainm an tuathanaich 's am baile gu robh thu dol. A h-ulle duine bha joba aige nuair a dh'fhag sinn Toronto. Chaidil mise 's a'chuid bu mhotha an oidhche sin an Toronto. Anns a'mhadainn chaidh mi slos chun a' 'railroad station' 's bha mi dol sios a Bhrampton – bha e miltean air falbh a Toronto an uair ud 's bha Seonaidh Shiurra comhla rium 's balach a mhuinntir nan Loch. Nuair a bha 'n triuir againn anns a 'rail-road station' thainig fear far an robh mis 's dh'fhoighnich e cait robh mi dol 's dh'inns mi gu robh mi dol sios gu Bhrampton. Dh'fhoighnich e co thige 's dh'inns mi dha 's thuirt c, o, gu robh tac mor alge. Thuirt e rium a dhol comhla ris 's thuirt mi de mu dheidhinn an da bhalach a bha comhla rium. Thuirt e gu robh tuathanaich gu leor timchioll air 's gu faigheadh iad joba. Chaidh sinn a mach 's chaidh Seonaidh Shiurra gu tuathanach a bha faisg dhomhs' 's chaidh fear na Loch sios bideag. Ach co chiubh, cha do dh'fhuirich mis' ach seachduinn aig an tuathanach agus chaidh sinn a steach gu Toronto a rithis. Thuirt mi ri Seonaidh Shiurra gu robh mi falbh's thuirt Seonaidh gu robh esain a'dol comhla rium.

'S dh'fhalbh sinn maduinn Di-luain gu Toronto 's fhuair sinn joba ann an sin a dhol dhan 'power house' – eadar Niagara Falls's Queenstown. Bha biadh math againn anns a'champ. Bha am biadh aig an tuathanach na b'fhearr na biadh a ghabh mise riamh. Bha mise anns an joba sin gu August. Chan fhaigheadh tu dha na States – bha quota ann man a tha fios agaibh agus 'on the 1st of

Donald 'Chrut' MacLeod and his great grandson Nicolas Scott Howe, Buffalo, 1986 (Courtesy Comunn Eachdraidh Nis)

July before the British quota was opened' – och, tha mi air a dhol dhan a'Bheurla rithist! Bha 'street-car' a'dol eadar Queensland 's Niagara Falls – bha e dol seachad air a'champ againne. Bhiodh sinn dol sios air a h-uile Di-Sathuirne gu Niagara Falls. Fhuair sinn a mach gu robh an quota a'fosgladh air 1st July's chaidh sinn gu Wharf an Emigration's fhuair sinn a null a sin.

Well, dh'fhuirich sinn mios eile aig an obair agus air 6th August thainig mise null air an abhainn dha na States. Bha mi da oidhche sin 's chaidh mi suas a Dhetroit agus bha mi ann an sin da bhliadhna 'g obair do Ford. Cheud gheamhradh bha sinn ag obair anns an 'shipyard' – bha lad a'togail an da phassenger boat bu mhotha bh'air na Lakes – sin 1923. As t-earrach, chaidh Seonaidh sios gu Niagara Falls a rithis 's chaidh mise gu Ford – cha b'ann, a samhradh sin bha mise 'g obair aig 'steel plant'. Thainig an geamhradh 's chaidh mi sios a Cleveland – an geamhradh 1923–24, bha mi ann an Cleveland. Bha torr de bhalaich Nis ann an uairsin cuideachd. Bha Lewis Society ann. Tha lad ag innse dhomhs nach eil ach aon bhalach a Leodhas ann an Cleveland an diugh. Bha timchioll air tri fichead ann an uair ud.

Dh'fhalbh mise as t-Earrach 's chaidh mi air na Lakes – mi-fhein 's Iain Mhurchaidh Mhoir a Suaineabost – a'Phoit. Chaidh sinn air na Lakes. Phos esain ann an Cleveland as deidh sin – chaidh mise Dhetroit – bha mi 'g obair aig Ford airson da bhliadhna. Chaldh Ford 'slack' an uairsin. Bha iad a'tionndadh 'from the old type to the new type of car' agus thainig mise nuas a Bhuffalo. Chaidh mi a dh'obair a Chevrolet plant there. Bha mi sin airson tri bliadhna agus as deidh sin phos mi. 'That was the end of my career, ha! ha!'

Nuair a landaig sinn ann a St Johns, New Brunswick 1923, chan fhaiceadh tu cail ach mullach 'freight sheds' – cha robh flos againn de seorsa ait' a bh'arm an Canada. Ach dol suas air an treine bho Montreal gu Toronto, cha robh moran ann an uair ud ach tacan. 'S e May a bh'ann 's bha sneachd air an talamh fhathast. Nuair a theann mise 'g obair aig a phower house, bha e gle mhath. Duine sam bith a chaidh a mach air a' *Mhetagama* bha obair aige ma bha e 'g iarraidh obair. Bha joba aige mas do dh'fhag e Toronto. Chaidh torr gu na tacan ach cha do dh'fhuirich iad gle fhada ann.

Bha cianalas air a h-uile duine dh'fhalbh a seo a'cheud mios neo dha. Ach bha h-uile duine og agus as deidh bliadhna na mar sin bha'n cianalas air falbh. Bha e gle mhath gun tainig iad 's sinne thoirt a mach a seo an uair ud. Cha robh cail a seo.

An fheadhainn a dh'fhalbh a'bhliadhna as deidh sin, cha do dh'fhuirich iad gle fhada thall ann. Ach duine sam bith a dh'fhalbh air a' *Mhetagama* – man a robh e ag obair, 's e choire fhein a bh'ann – cheud bhliadhna. 'S nuair a chaidh mise Dhetroit bha obair gu leor an sin ma bha thu airson obair.

An tuathanach gun deach mise, bha e cho gasd ri duine chunna tu riamh – gu h-araid i fhein, bha e gle mhath dhomhs. Bha thu sguir a dh'obair agus bha h-uile duine dol dhan eaglais La-na-

Sabaid. Bha na daoine gle mhath. Bhiodh sinn a'faighinn litrichean bho'n tigh. Bha sinn a'faighinn litir a h-uile darna seachduinn co dhiubh. Bhiodh iad a'faighinn litrichean aig an tigh – fhios agad, bha coir agad fuireach aig an tuathanach gus am paidheadh tu do phassage. Fhuair a h-uile duine a bha sud a mach gun chail – cha do phaidh duine dol air a' *Mhetagama*. Agus fhuair m'athair litir a'foighneach cait an robh mi 's nach do dh'fhuirich mi aig an tuathanach. Bha chuid as motha faighinn sin. Ach as deidh speil – 'they forgot about it'. Bha iad airson do thoirt a mach a seo 's bha fios aca gle mhath nach robh chuid bu mhotha dol a dh'fhuireach aig an tuathanach. Ach 's e sinn thoirt a mach a seo 's ar cur a Chanada 's e sin a 'main thing'. 'Both governments had an agreement' – gu faigheadh lad na daoine og a mach a Leodhas. Bha cus ann 's cha robh obair ann – cha robh e dona, cha robh e dona idir.

Nam biodh Leodhas an uair ud man a tha e an diugh, cha chan fhalbhadh duine ann. Carson a dh'fhalbhadh iad? Tha e cheart cho math ri aite th'ann an Amearacaidh neo 'n Canada an diugh. Chan eil bailtean cho mor ach tha thu cheart cho math dheth ged a bhiodh tu 'n Canada. Ach 57 years ago, cha robh cail ann. Duine ag obair aig an ola an diugh a'faighinn ann an aon seachduinn barrachd airgiod na bh'ann an Nis gu leir nuair a dh'fhalbh mis' as. Bola min an uair ud, cha robh e cosg ach sia tasdain dheug – an diugh fichead not, tha mi creids. Cha robh airgiod ann. Chan iarrainn air duine sam bith emigratadh as a seo an diugh.

Bha Gaelic Society ann agus a h-uile mios bhiodh sinn a'coinneachadh agus a'gabhail amhrain 's a'danns. Oidhche Shathuirne gu timchioll air leth uair an deidh aon-uairdeug. Bha e gle mhath. Chuld as motha as a h-uile baile, bhiodh iad ri dol ann. Blia Society mor againn ann an Detroit. Bha fear ann as Aignish – 's e am President a bh'ann, agus bha e ann airson bliadhnachan as deidh sin. Bhiodh na ceudan dol chun Lewis Society ann an Detroit an uair ud. Chaneil moran dhiubh ann an diugh ach an te tha'n Detroit, tha i gle mhath fhathast. Bha te mhath againn ann an Cleveland, ach chan eil ach aon duine a Leodhas beo ann an Cleveland an diugh – as aithne dhomhs. An uair ud ann an Cleveland, bha Domhnull Gheadaidh, Ruairidh Timid, mi-fhein, Seonaidh Shiurra, Murchadh Timid, Seonaidh Thirty a Eoropaidh, Calum Iain Buachaill a Eoropaidh, A'Phoit, Doilidh Dhomhnuill

Mhurchaidh Iain, Cows a Cros, Coinneach a'Phoc – bha fear a mhuinntir, a'Phuirt 's chan eil fhios de dh'eirich dha. Dh'fhalbh e as t-Earrach 's cha chuala iad a riamh mu dheidhinn as deidh sud. Bha da phiuthair aige ann a Chicago cuideachd. Bha iadsan a riamh a'feuchainn ri faighinn a mach cait an deach e. Bha Niall Siamalan ann cuideachd a Lianal agus torr a Steornabhagh's bho'n Bhac agus as a Rubha. Bha tri fichead ann as a'gheamhradh ud 's chan eil moran aca an diugh air an talamh. 'S bha Society ac' ann am Buffalo nuair a chaidh mi ann. 'S e Aonghas a'Bhostaidh am President a bh'againn. Chan eil ach sianar a Nis ann an diugh. Bha da fhichead uaireigin ann.

Lewis Society of Cleveland, Ohio, 6 April 1925. Back row (left to right): Donald Macleod,* Swainbost; John Mackenzie, Europie; Malcolm McIver, Back; Hector McInnes, North Tolsta; Finlay Morrison, Ardbrock. Second back row (left to right): John Ferguson, Back; Wallace Nicholson, Dell; Murdo Smith, Europie; Donald MacLeod, Point; Donald MacLeod, Point; Malcom MacRitchie, Point. Centre row (left to right):Donald MacLeod, Back; John MacDonald,* Europie; Malcolm MacRitchie, Lionel; Angus MacDonald.* Europie; Malcolm Morrison, Europie; Donald MacDonald, Lionel. Second from row (left to right): Donald McLeod, Back; Angus Campbell, Lionel; Norman MacLeod, Ardbrock; Donald MacDonald, Back-Foreman; Roderick Smith, Europie; Donald MacLeod, Europie; Angus MacDonald, Port of Ness. Front row (left to right): Kenneth MacLeod, Swainbost; Donald MacLean, Swainbost; John McRitchie, Swainbost; MacLeod, Cross, Ness; McIver, Point.

* Interviewed. Names and photograph supplied by Angus MacDonald

Murchadh Domhnullach (Courtesy Cominn Eachdraidh Nis)

## *Murchadh Domhnullach*

*Ness*

*Comunn Eachonaidh Nis 1980*

'S ANN AN April 1923 a dh'fhalbh sinn air a' *Metagama*. Bha seisear againn as a'bhaile agus 's e bus beag le John Mitchell a thug a Steornabhagh sinn. Bha da cheud duine oirr' as an eilean. Chaidh sinn a mach air tender. Bha e aig acair air taobh mulgh an Tigh Sholais. Nuair a dh'fhalbh sinn, rinn e air a'Phort agus bha e ann a sin aig tuiteam na h-oidhche. Bha teine mor ann am borgh agus cha robh duine as a sgire nach robh ann. Nuair a bha e dol seachad am bagh, sheid e a chonocag. Cha robh cail an corr ann gus na rainig sinn St John. 'S ann a Qhuebec a bha sinn supposed a dhol ach thachair an deigh ruinn agus chaidh sinn a St John. Bha sinn le hold-up againn da latha ann a sin. Bha flood ann agus mhill e a railway. Chaidh sinn suas gu Toronto agus chaidh pairt againn a chur a mach ann a sin. Ach chaidh mise agus balaich a'bhaile chur gu London, Ontario. Bha na tuathanaich a'feitheamh ruinn ann a sin agus chaidh a h-uile fear dha aite fhein.

Bha mise aig tuathanach airson naoi miosan – an tuathanach, 's a bhean, balach m'aois fhein (22 years), agus Nighean dol dhan a sgoil. Bha sgoil ceither mile air falbh. Bha car aca agus nuair a bha sneachd ann 's e horse and buggy a bhiodh aca. Brick house a bh'ann. Bha gu leoir obair ann agus bha gu leoir biadh. Aig an am sin cha robh am paigheadh gle mhor – £5 a month. 'S e general farming a bha ann le crodh 's caoraich is bha apple orchard ann. Bhiodh am balach a'toirt na h-ubhlan gu marcaid a London.

Nuair a dh'fhalbh mi as a sin, chaidh mi London, Ontario, agus bha mi ag obair ann a sin aig a' Chanadian National Railway gu an ath shamhraidh agus 's ann ann a sin a thachair Tarmod Iain Ailean rium. Chaidh sinn suas gu aite ris an can iad Wallaceburgh – baile beag. Fhuair sinn obair ann a sugar factory. Bha sinn corr is bliadhna 'g obair ann a sin. Nuair a dh'fhalbh sinn as a sin chaidh sinn a null dhan na States agus chun na Lakes. Cha d'fhuair sinn air an aon bhata. Bha mi seoladh air na Lakes gun tainig mi dhachaidh ann a 1935.

# *Summary*

The *Metagama* emigration can be seen both as a significant event in Lewis history and as a media phenomenon of the twentieth century.

For more than one hundred years, country folk from all over Britain and, indeed, Europe had removed to the cities and the New World. The Gaels, however, in their determination to keep issues of land and culture to the forefront, effectively fought a rearguard action, the success of which, particularly in the 1880s and early 1920s, made Lewis a place of some interest to the nation's press. The fact that her people were then seen to be slightly out of step with the fashion-consciousness of the new order heightened this interest, and the prospect of a twentieth-century Highland clearance opening the floodgates to a new wave of British emigration made a media deluge inevitable.

Both civil service conspiracies and cheap labour have their admirers, but the fact that Lewis people were given preferential treatment in this emigration scheme is also significant. It is my belief that many Canadians were able to look beyond the hyperbolae, to the intrinsic value of Gaelic culture in the hope that, by giving priority to, acquiring what Britain apparently wanted rid off, they might somehow improve their own society.

James Shaw Grant has a good line, that Gaeldom has traditionally been viewed by others 'through the wrong end of a telescope' and, instead of being an anachronism, is somehow a portent. I like that. Not a quaint and distant civilisation in need of improvement or modernisation, but a culture close to oneself and, inasmuch as it retains principles of morality and equality, perhaps a model for the future. Mr Grant, of course, has held the 'prosbaig' in his own hands on occasion, and recently (1976) advocated legislative change in favour of individual croft ownership.

Some interesting patterns emerge from the interviews. Most emigrants made marriages with fellow Leosachs whom they usually met through the network of Lewis and Gaelic societies or the Gaelic Church, and the Church itself appears to have assumed a growing importance in people's lives. Many were converted in the 1920s and 1930s and most survivors retain strong links with Presbyterian churches. This subject, I feel, would be worth further study.

Virtually all depended upon Lewis connections in finding employment and accommodation in North America, and most of the men tended to gravitate towards the water in their search for a working environment in which they felt most at ease. The seasonal nature of this work brought the traditionally sought-after variety.

Curiously, pieces of paper acquired a new importance in their lives – boarding cards, seamen's tickets, immigration documents and so forth. Whereas in the old country if you didn't have a scrap of *land* your prospects were restricted, in the New World it sometimes seemed that if you didn't have the appropriate scrap of *paper* your life could be similarly blighted.

This, then, was the lot of the *Metagama* emigrant – a life shaped in two places, by two sets of circumstances, two types of experience. Was the emigration desirable or necessary, and, if so, to whom? Personally I deplore the secret negotiations by which the Government attempted to deprive people of their birthright, but what other useful conclusion can one reach? Lewismen and women have traditionally reserved the right to see the world and create their own little bit of the Eilean an Fhraoich wherever they saw fit, and, if my experience is anything to go by, some of the far-flung corners of the earth are better places as a result. But then, is Lewis commensurately poorer? At least having paid the price, the people of Lewis have demonstrated a rare ability to get something in return.

# *APPENDIX I – Shipping List*
*(Metagama)*

*Stornoway Gazette*: Thursday, April 26, 1923

**List of Lewis emigrants** (left Saturday, April 21, 1923, on *Metagama*)

**Cameron** – Murdo, 28 Aird of Tong*; Angus, 28 Aird of Tong

**Campbell** – Angus, 10 New Garrabost; Kenneth, 15 Arnol Barvas; Angus, 15 Branahuie; Roderick, 10 Upper Garrabost; Malcolm, 18 Garrabost

**Clarke** – Archibald N., 3 Matheson Road, Stornoway

**Conning** – David, 17 Keith Street, Stornoway

**Crichton** – Kenneth, 6 Aignish; Donald, 11 Swordale

**Ferguson** – Donald, 22 Laxay, Lochs

**Finlayson** – Norman, 11 Brue, Barvas; Murdo, 43 Newton Street, Stornoway

**Graham** – Malcolm, 6 New Garrabost;* Mary, Lighthill, Back; Alex M., 4 Holm; Murdo, 20 Coll, Back; Alex, 14 Melbost; Kenneth, 14 Melbost; William, 5 Coll, Back*

**Grant** – Donald, 5 Laxdale Lane, Stornoway

**Gunn** – Malcolm, 11 Port of Ness

**Kennedy** – John, 2 Calbost, Lochs; Hector S., 38 Leurbost, Lochs; Kenneth J., 42 Point Street, Stornoway; Alex D., 42 Point Street, Stornoway; John, 4 Cromore, Lochs; Maggie, 2 Calbost, Lochs*

**Kerr** – Alex J., 64 Keith Street, Stornoway

**Logan** – Rena F., 57 Inaclete Road, Stornoway

**MacArthur** – Kenneth, 32 Upper Carloway; Donald J., 4 Tolsta Chaolais; Alex, 16 Sheshader; Kenneth, 14 Port of Ness; Murdo, 9 Sheshader Point

**MacAskill** – Norman, 12 Portnaguran; Mabel, 20 East Street, Sandwick; Donald, 20 Gravir, Lochs

**MacAulay** – John, 56 North Shawbost; Roderick, 22 Shader Point

**MacDonald** – S., Aird Dell, Ness; John, 2 Brue, Barvas; Donald, 19 Cromore, Lochs; Roderick, H., 9 Battery Park, Stornoway; Donald, 4 Park, Barvas; Angus, 27 Eoropie, Ness;* Finlay, 20 Aignish;* John, 16 Eoropie, Ness;* John, 35 Arnol Barvas; Kenneth, 22 Shader Point; Donald, 30 Swordale Point; Murdo, 5 Port of Ness;* Angus, 23 Cromore, Lochs; John G., 2 Scotland Street, Stornoway; Donald, 26 Aignish; Finlay, 25 Habost, Ness;* Angus, 57 South Bragar;* John, 4 Reef, Uig; George, 11 Sheshader Point; William John, North End, Keose; Duncan, 23 Lower Sandwick; Angus, 18 Kipper Road, Stornoway; Angus, 17 Knockaird, Ness;* Angus, Aird Dell, Ness; William, 32 Newton, Stornoway

**MacFarlane** – Murdo, 26 Melbost;* Angus, 4 Port of Ness

**MacGregor** – Donald, 6 Shader Point

**MacInnes** – John, 31 Goathill Cottages, Stornoway; Norman, 24 Achmore; Jessie A., 20 Achmore

**MacIver** – Norman, 37 New Park, Laxdale; Norman, 45 North Shawbost; Colin, 4 Melbost;* Donald A., 45 North Shawbost; Angus, 20 Lower Bayble; John, 41 Coll; James, 27 Swordale; Donald A, 17 Shader Point; Alex, 23 Aignish; Kenneth, 1 Vatisker, Back; Ian, Seaforth House; Angus, 17 Shader Point; Donald, 5 Tong Park; Archibald, 20 Newton; Alex, 8 Benside; Donald, 45 New Park, Bayble; Norman, 3 Aird Point*

**MacKay** – Angus, 7 North Bragar; Kenneth, 10 Arnol Barvas; Malcolm, 24 South Shawbost; John, 8 High Borve; Donald, 11 Eoropie, Ness; Roderick, 31 Keith Street, Stornoway; Donald, 20 Arnol Barvas; John, 35 Aird Tong; Angus, 14 Upper Garrabost; Donald, 1 Kenneth Street, Stornoway

**MacKinnon** – Allan, 15 Kenneth Street, Stornoway; Kenneth, 8 Ranish, Lochs

**MacKenzie** – Mary A., 35 North Street, Sandwick; Donald, Thule House, Port of Ness; John, 11 Eoropie, Ness;* Angus, 33 Eoropie, Ness;* Alex, 36 Back; Alastair, 1 Aird, Uig; Harry, 18 Plantation Road, Stornoway; James M., Granite House, Stornoway; Donald, 16 Port of Ness; Donald, 9 Knock Point; Donald, 51 Coll; Duncan, 15 Laxay, Lochs; John, 7 Aird Tong; Roderick, 12 Crossbost; Roderick, 23 Upper Bayble

**MacLean** – John, 10 North Bragar; Donald, 24 Swainbost, Ness;* Murdo, 10 Portnaguran; Alex, 11 Sand Street, Coulregrein; Cathie, 2 Bells Road, Stornoway; Donald, 4 Lionel; Donald, 30 New Shawbost; John, 24 North Shawbost; Alex, 39 Leurbost; John, 18 South Bragar; John, 30 Coll, Back; Angus, 28 Breasclete; Alex, 60 Keith Street, Stornoway

**MacLennan** – Duncan, 1 East Street, Sandwick; Murdo, 10 Fivepenny; Donald, 36 North Tolsta

**MacLeod** – John, 11 Swainbost, Ness;* Donald, 4 Vatisker, Back; Kenneth, 12 North Shawbost; Donald, 20 New Shawbost; Norman, 7 Aignish;* Roderick, Golf House, Stornoway; Murdo, 27 Keith Street, Stornoway; George, 8 Crossbost; Maggie, 33 Aird Tong; Johanna, 37 Lower Bayble; Chirsty, 12 Cross, Ness; Christina, 34 South Beach, Stornoway;* Murdo, 5 New Shawbost; William J., 19 Knock Point; John, 17 Ranish, Lochs; John, 11 Upper Garrabost; Allan, 15 Lower Bayble; Donald, 28 Swainbost;* Murdo, 8 Borrowston, Carloway; Kenneth, 12 North Shawbost; Norman, 10 Borrowston, Carloway; Angus, 21 North Shawbost; James R., 4 Sand Street, Coulregrein; Kenneth, 29 Lower Bayble; John, 49 Back; Angus, 54 Coll, Back; Roderick, 3 Barnahuie; Donald, 8 Knockaird, Ness;* Malcolm, 34 Eoropie, Ness; James, 8 Calbost, Lochs; Donald, 10 Balallan; Donald, 63 Coll, Back;* James, 33 Aird Tong;* Malcolm, 8 Coll, Back; Donald, 12 Goathill Cottages, Stornoway; Murdina, 14 Steinish; John M., 27 Laxay, Lochs; Malcolm, 27 Laxay, Lochs; Peter, 17 Swordale Point; Malcolm, 5 Ranish; Donald, 8 Crossbost; Neil, School Street, Vatisker; Murdo, 1 Ranish; Malcolm, 42 Ranish; Peter, 37 Point Street, Stornoway; Donald, 13 Branahuie; Roderick, 4 Upper Garrabost; Angus, 5 Lower Sandwick; Murdo A., 1 New Valley; Donald John, 4 Laxdale Lane; Donald, 5b North Tolsta; Donald, 10 Aird Tong

**MacMillan** – Colin, 14 Aignish

**MacPhail** – Alex D., 9 Laxdale; Donald A., 6 MacKenzie Street, Stornoway; Colin, 33 Upper Carloway; Malcolm, 32 North Bragar

**MacRae** – John, 42 Lower Bayble; Angus, Goathill Farm, Stornoway; George, 5 Grimshader

**MacRitchie** – John, 5 Swainbost, Ness;* Angus, 2 North Dell, Ness;* Angus N., 2 North Dell, Ness*

**MacSween** – Roderick, 7 Laxdale Lane

**Martin** – John, 33 Lower Shader; Murdo, 15 Leurbost, Lochs

**Matheson** – Isabelle, 37 Kenneth Street, Stornoway; William, 4 Brue, Barvas; John M., Marybank, Stornoway; John, 6 Flesherin Point; Murdo, 10 Aird Tong

**Montgomery** – Angus, 10 Bells Road, Stornoway; Donald, 16 Ranish; Donald, 9 Garrabost; Catherine, 50 Keith Street, Stornoway; John, 6 Sheshader Point; Donald, 36 Ranish, Lochs; Murdo, 43 New Market, Stornoway;* Chrissie, 43 New Market, Stornoway*

**Morrison** – Roderick, 4 South Dell, Ness; Alex, 6 North Dell, Ness; Helen, 46 North Shawbost; Roderick, 22 New Shawbost; Malcolm, 10 Eoropie, Ness;* Donald, 23 Fivepenny; Alex, 21 Upper Shader; Donald, 35 Lionel, Ness; John, 46 North Shawbost; Norman, 26 Habost, Ness; Alex, 14 Back; Murdo, 22 Knock Carloway; John, 11 Lionel, Ness; Norman, 13 Reef, Uig; John, Well House, Back; Norman, 54 Keith Street, Stornoway; Malcolm, 7 Lower Shader, Barvas

**Murray** – Mary, 6 New Shawbost; Kenneth, 43 South Shawbost; Alex, 42 South Shawbost; Lewis, 42 Point Street, Stornoway; Murdo, 31 New Park, Knock

**Munro** – Murdo, 19 Lower Sandwick; Norman, 19 Lower Sandwick; Alex, 20 Branahuie

**Nicolson** – Finlay, 11 Knock Point; William, 2 Benside; Hector, Helm Farm: John, 11 Calbost, Lochs

**Paterson** – Neil, 20 Brue, Barvas

**Rennie** – Bessie R, Tong School*

**Ross** – Robert, 51 Bayhead Street, Stornoway

**Simpson** – Malcolm, Tong, Stornoway

**Smith** – John, 5 Knock, Carloway; Roderick, 1 Aignish; Donald, North Dell, Ness; Roderick, 4 Eoropie, Ness;* Malcolm, 5 North Bragar;* John, Park, Borve; Angus, 24 Breasclete; Angus, 5 North Bragar;* John, 32 Upper Bayble; Norman J., 5 North Bragar;* John M., 5 North Bragar;* Malcolm, 15 North Beach Street, Stornoway; Donald, 31 Leurbost

**Steven** – Thomas, 12 Seaview Terrace, Stornoway

**Stewart** – Alexander, 26 Coll, Back
**Thomson** – Evander, 16 Aird Tong*

*Interviewed, photographed or mentioned in text

From a total figure of 260 (242 men and 18 women) the place of origin of the *Metagama* emigrants breaks down as follows:

| | |
|---|---|
| 1. Point District | 20.8% |
| 2. Stornoway (Town) | 13.8% |
| 3. Ness | 13.5% |
| 4. Tong–Tolsta | 12.7% |
| 5. Lochs | 10.8% |
| 6. West Side | 10.8% |
| 7. Barvas District | 8.8% |
| 8. Stornoway (Townships) | 8.8% |

or 14% urban, 8.6% rural, which was roughly in proportion to the population distribution of the island.

STORNOWAY HARBOUR

| Date of Entry | | Ship | Master | Port of Registry | Reg. Tonnage | Whence Arrived | Cargo Landed | Consignee or Agent | Cargo Shipped | Shipper or Agent | Destination | Date of Departure | | Folio | Remarks |
|---|---|---|---|---|---|---|---|---|---|---|---|---|---|---|---|
| Apl | 10 | Explorer S/S | | | | Cruising | | Captain | — | — | — | Apl | 10 | — | to Tows Water |
| | . | Eilean Glas | Cunningham | Stornoway | 36 | Leverburgh | [illegible] ✓ | [illegible] | General ✓ | E. Mackenzie | Oline | ✓ | 11 | [illegible] | |
| | 10 | Sheila S/S | Cameron | Glasgow | 97 | Kyle | Mails ✓ | D. McBrayne Ltd | Mails ✓ | D. McBrayne Ltd | Kyle | . | 11 | 235 | |
| | 11 | Sheila S/S | Cameron | Glasgow | 97 | Kyle | Mails ✓ | D° | Mails ✓ | D° | Kyle | . | 12 | 235 | |
| | 12 | Sheila S/S | Cameron | Glasgow | 97 | Kyle | Mails ✓ | D° | Mails ✓ | D° | Kyle | | 13 | 235 | |
| | 13 | [illegible] | [illegible] | [illegible] | 602 | Wick | — | W. Leverhulme Ltd | [illegible] | W. Leverhulme Ltd | [illegible] | | 15 | 235 | |
| | . | Sheila S/S | Cameron | Glasgow | 97 | Kyle | Mails ✓ | D. McBrayne Ltd | Mails ✓ | D. McBrayne Ltd | Kyle | | 16 | 235 | |
| | 15 | Glentaise S/S | McCalmont | Belfast | 512 | East Coast | General ✓ | M. Maclean | General ✓ | M. Maclean | Belfast | | [illegible] | 235 | |
| | 16 | Rose S/S | [illegible] | [illegible] | [illegible] | Inverness | Coals ✓ | [illegible] | — | — | — | | [illegible] | — | |
| | . | Sheila S/S | Cameron | Glasgow | 97 | Kyle | Mails ✓ | D. McBrayne Ltd | Mails ✓ | D. McBrayne Ltd | Kyle | | [illegible] | 235 | |
| | 17 | Rebecca S/S | Boyd | Glasgow | 115 | Glasgow | General ✓ | D° | General ✓ | D° | Glasgow | | [illegible] | 236 | |
| | . | Sheila S/S | Cameron | Glasgow | 97 | Kyle | Mails ✓ | D° | Mails ✓ | D° | Kyle | | 18 | 236 | |
| | 18 | Ellen & Irene | Maclean | Stornoway | 42 | | — | D. MacLeod | Furniture ✓ | D. MacLeod | Gairloch | | 18 | — | [illegible] |
| | . | Sheila S/S | Cameron | Glasgow | 97 | Kyle | Mails ✓ | D. McBrayne Ltd | Mails ✓ | D. McBrayne Ltd | Kyle | | 19 | 236 | |
| | . | Jan S/S | McCallum | Stornoway | 39 | Glasgow | Coals ✓ | D. McLean Ltd | — | — | — | | 19 | — | |
| | 19 | Sheila S/S | Cameron | Glasgow | 97 | Kyle | Mails ✓ | D. McBrayne Ltd | Mails ✓ | D. McBrayne Ltd | Kyle | | 20 | 236 | |
| | 20 | Sheila S/S | Cameron | Glasgow | 97 | Kyle | Mails ✓ | D° | Mails ✓ | D° | Kyle | | 21 | 236 | |
| | . | Jane S/S | McCallum | Stornoway | 39 | Badcaul | Fish ✓ | D. McLean Ltd | — | — | — | | 23 | 236 | |
| | 21 | Hebrides S/S | Campbell | Glasgow | 236 | Tarbert | — | M. Maclean | — | — | — | | 21 | — | |
| | . | Metagama S/S | Turnbull | London | 7655 | Glasgow | — | M. Maclean | Passengers [illegible] | M. Maclean | Quebec | | 21 | | Embarked 310 Passengers for Canada |
| | 22 | Glentaise S/S | McCalmont | Belfast | 612 | Belfast | General ✓ | D° | General ✓ | M. Maclean | East Coast | | 23 | 236 | |
| | 23 | Rebecca S/S | Boyd | Glasgow | 115 | Glasgow | General ✓ | D. McBrayne Ltd | General ✓ | D. MacBrayne Ltd | Glasgow | | 22 | 236 | |
| | . | Sheila S/S | Cameron | Glasgow | 97 | Kyle | Mails ✓ | D° | Mails ✓ | D° | Kyle | | 24 | 236 | |
| | 24 | Sheila S/S | Cameron | Glasgow | 97 | Kyle | Mails ✓ | D° | Mails ✓ | D° | Kyle | | 26 | 236 | |
| | 25 | Sheila S/S | Cameron | Glasgow | 97 | Kyle | Mails ✓ | D° | Mails ✓ | D° | Kyle | | 26 | 236 | |
| | | | | Glasgow | 97 | Kyle | Mails ✓ | D° | Mails ✓ | D° | Kyle | | 27 | 236 | |
| | | | | Belfast | 423 | East Coast | General ✓ | M. Maclean | General ✓ | M. Maclean | Belfast | | 27 | 236 | |
| | | | | Glasgow | 97 | Kyle | Mails ✓ | D. McBrayne Ltd | Mails ✓ | D. McBrayne | Kyle | | 28 | 236 | |
| | | | | | | | | [illegible] | — | — | — | May | [illegible] | — | |

Extracts from the Stornoway Harbour Commission Register, April 1923

Silver Goblet – a souvenir of the *Metagama*, found in a Toronto shipping office by Captain John MacDonald (Lewis and Toronto)

# *APPENDIX II – Songs*

## Saoil an till mi chaoidh

Saoil an till mi chaoidh dha na glinn 'san robh mi òg,
Far 'm bu chridheil aoibhneach sinn gun uallach irmtirm oirnn;
A' buachailleachd crodh-laoigh agus gamhna mar bu nòs,
An till mise chaoidh dha na glinn 's an robh mi òg?

'S minig mi a'beachdachadh air na h-achaibh 's iad fo phòr,
Fraoch gu bàrr nam beannaibh is na machraichean fo ròs;
Eathraichean ag iasgach is cuid sgiamhach ruith fo sheòl,
'S a'ghrian ri dol sios taobh an Iar Loch-a-Ròg.

Cha dèan mise dìochuimhn 'air feasgar feathach reòit'
An eala bhàn 'na sgiamha ri sgiathalaich 'san òs;
A' ghealach cho ion-mhiannaichte ri riaghladh anns na neòil,
Is fuaim Tràigh Uig is Shanndaig – O, b'annsa leam an ceòl.

Ged a ruiginn crìochan air fad 's air leud nan stàit'
M' aigne-sa bidh 'g iarraidh do'n àit 's an dèanainn tàmh
Far bheil na beanntan fianaich 's an sliabh fo chaoraich bhlàr,
'S far an cluinn thu 'n Cuan-a-Siar tighinn gu h-iarganach gu
    tráigh.

Ged is fhada thall tha mi 's gun ghanntachd air mo stòr,
Tha mo dhùrachd-sa measg ghleanntan is bheanntan Eilean
    Leòdhais,
Ach tha sùil agam bhith ann roimh fheasgarfann mo lò,
Is Lùiginn a bhith adhiaichte aig Ceann Tràigh Dhaile Móir.

Mo bheannachd leis gach mathair tha 's na làithean so ri bròn
Airson dealachadh ri pàisdean, is pàirt nach tachair beò;
'S eagal leam gum fàsaichear àit' mo ghràidh rinn m'àrach òg:
Na dh'fhag am *Metagàma* ac' tha 'm *Marloch* leò fo sheòl.

*Malcolm Macleod (Calum Fox) Garenin*

*This song was composed in Detroit, USA, about 1925. Author returned home in ill health about 1927, died in 1930, and is buried in Dalmore, as he had wished.*

*Courtesy: Songs of Eilean nan Fhraoich*

## Eilean beag donn a'chuain

*Seisd*

Hì-ri-o-rì, togaidh sinn form
Air Eilean beag donn a'chuain,
Eilean beag Leódhais dachaidh nan seòid
A chumas a' chòmhrag suas;
Eilean nan tonn, a dh'àraich na suirm
'S a chuidich an Fhraing gu buaidh,
Còmhla ri chéile togaidh sinn form
Air Eilean beag donn a'chuain.

Bha Ghearmailt ealamh's i sealladh mu'n Iar
'S an domhain ma b'fhior 'na dòrn;
A rùn air cogadh 's i togail a sàth
De chaistealan àlainn ceò;
Clach-stéidh am bunait air gainneamh na tràgh'd,
Am mullach gu h-àrd 's na neòil –
'S earball-sàil na h-Iuthairn a h-àit'
'Nuair thig am muir-làn 'na còir.

A Dhia bi maille ri muinntir a' bhròin,
'S na fir a tha leòinte, tinn,
Bho ìnean guineach na h-oilair' a bhòc
Air fuil agus feòil do chloinn;
Tha gaoth an fhir-mhillidh 'na itean, 's a chròg
A' druideadh m'a sgòrnan teann,
Tha'n leómhann a' fasgadh Uilleam a Dhà
Is spiollaidh i chnàmhan lom.

Do làmh, a charaid, do dh'Eilean a' chuain
'S a h-eallach cho cruaidh is trom,
Tha'm bàs 'na chabhaig ri sgathadh's a' buain,
Gun duine ni suas an call;
Tha'n òigridh sgoinneil a shòlas na caoil
An àite na laoich a bh'ann,
Gun bhoineid, gun bhròig, a' siubhal an raoin
An Eilean an Fhraoich ud thall.

O's làidir na bannan 'g am tharruing a null
Gu eilean beag donn Mhicleòid,

'S gu stiùir mi gu h-ealamh gu cala mo long
'Nuair ruigeas mi ceann mo lò;
'S ma ghreimicheas m'acair ri Carraig nan Al
Bidh m'anam tighinn sàbhailt beò,
Mo shiùill air am pasgadh am fasgadh Chill'-Sgàir,
Le m'athair's mo mhàthair chòir.

*By Donald Morrison (Dòmhnull 'an Moireasdan) Bragar and Duluth. Died Duluth 1951.*

*Courtesy: Songs of Eilean nan Fhraoich.*

**Do na h-Eileanaich air a'** ***Mhetagama***
le Iain Stiubhart, Coll, Leodhas

Comunn Eachdraidh Nis

Tha sinne nochd cho cianail, truagh
'S chan ioghnadh ged a tha
A 'cuimhneachadh nan ceudan laoch
Rinn triall uainn thar an t-sal
Is ged is mor a'bheannachd e
Gun dhealaich iad 'nan slaint
Cha leighis sin air taobh seach taobh
Na cridheachan tha sgainnt.

Cha nar leam ged a dh'aidichinn
Nuair sheall mi mach am Braigh
'S a chunnaic mi 'n long ud 's i
A 'seòladh sios air fair'
Gun dh'fhairich mi de chianalas
Na shil mi sios gu lar
Nuair smaoinich mi nach coinnichinn
Ri cuid aca gu brath.

Chan e mhain an t-aite seo
An drasda tha fo ghruaim
Bha buidheann as gach cearnaidh innt'
O'n airde deas in tuath

'S ged nach biodh daimh no cairdean innt'
Tha craidh ann a tha cruaidh
An duthaich bhi 'ga fasachadh
De na bh'innte bharr an t-sluaigh.

Tha'n tir tha seo gu fasachadh
'S tha sin ga 'm fhagail tinn
Tha 'm bith-beo bu ghnathach di
Air fas cho gann 'nar linn
'S gu feum sinn uile fagail 's dol
Do chearnaidhean tha thall.
An duil ri cuis na's fabharaich
'S an aite tha seo cho mall.

Nuair chuimhnich sinn na bliadhnaichean
Bha'n t-iasgach na mhor ard
Na Miltean is na ceudan 's iad
A'triall thuig' as gach cearn
'S nuair thigeadh crioch nan iasgaichean
'S a philleadh iad g'an ait
Gum biodh an corr de'n bhliadhn' aca
Gun fhriamh le 'n sporran saitht'.

Tha sinne cho gearr-sheallach dall
'Nar breithnichean co dhiubh
Chan eil sinn idir caithriseach
Mar chaitheas sinn ar n-uin'
Oir tirean beartach dh'fhasaich E
Air sgath mor lochd an t-sluaigh
'S cha teid sinn as mar aicheadh sinn
Ar doighean grannda thruaigh.

Is ged tha Dia toirt peanais air
A shamhuil se de dh'ait
Gidheadh tha E lan aithreachais
Nam pilleamaid 'na thrath
Nam bith bitheamaid air ar n-urnhlachadh
'Nar cridh 's ar gluin air lar
Thiomidaidheadh E gach freasdal teann
'S bhiodh saobhir dhuinn le ghras.

Co dhiubh tha sinn fo chianalas
Bho'n thriall iad as gach ait'
An comunn chleachd bhi maille ruinn
M'an teine h-uile la
Bhiodh Aonghas is da Dhomhmall ann
Co dhiubh 's mur tigeadh cach
'S e'n 'Geamhradh' bhiodh an comhnuidh ac'
Na'n togta fonn gu h-ard.

'S e'n 'Geamhradh' bh'ort mar fhar-ainm
Ach chaidh do bhaisteadh cearr
Cha robh fiu neach bho aineoil ort
Nach mothaicheadh do bhlaths.
'S a riamh o fhair mi eolas ort
'S tu comhla rium ri d'cheard
Gu'n d'fhuair thu ait am aignidhean
Nach caraich as gu brath.

Ach tha sinn uile dochasach
Ma bhios sinn beo le cheil'
Nuair gheibh na laoich de storas
Na ni doigheal iad gu leir
Gun tig iad cuairt a shealltuinn oirnn
A nall do'n tir seo fein
'S ma thig bheir mis mo lamhas dhaibh
Gu'm faigh iad failt d'a reir.

Tha nis mo sgil mar bhard an seo
An drasd air ruith gu ceann
Cha robh mi riamh ri bardachd
Oir cha b'e mo cheard a bh'ann

Ach eisdibh, o mo chairdean,
Ged tha faillnigidhean ann
Tha sgil gu leoir aig pairt agaibh
'S na fagaibh rann dhith cam.

An Uig wedding in Detroit, Murdanie MacLeod and Peggy MacLennan

No. [illegible]

# Marriage License

193 2

## Wayne County, Michigan

**To any person legally authorized to solemnize marriage,**

## Greeting:

**Marriage May Be Solemnized Between**

Mr. Murdanie MacLeod and M Peggy MacLennan, affidavit having been filed in this office, as provided by Public Act No. 128, Laws of 1887, as amended, by which it appears that said

Murdanie MacLeod is 29 years of age, color is white, residence is Detroit, Michigan, and birthplace was Scotland, occupation is auto worker, father's name Donald, and mother's maiden name was Isabella has been previously married no time s; and that said Peggy MacLennan is 31 years of age, color is white residence is Detroit, Michigan and birthplace was Scotland occupation is waitress, father's name Murdo, and mother's maiden name was Annie Macaulay and who has been previously married no time s, and whose maiden name was ______, and whose ______ Parent's or Guardian's consent, in case she has not attained the age of eighteen years, has been filed in my office.

**In Witness Whereof,** I have hereunto attached my hand and the seal of Wayne County, Michigan, this 12th day of September A. D. 193 2.

L. S.

Thos. F. Farrell
County Clerk
by Chas. A. [illegible]
Deputy Clerk

HP

## Certificate of Marriage

Between Mr. Murdanie MacLeod and M Peggy MacLennan

**I hereby certify** that, in accordance with the above license, the persons herein mentioned were joined in marriage by me, at Detroit, County of Wayne, Michigan, on the 22nd day of September A. D. 1932, in the presence of Isabella MacLeod, of Detroit, and Donald Morrison, of Detroit, as witnesses.

Roy L. Aldrich
Name of Magistrate or clergyman.

Minister
Official Title

**THIS DUPLICATE** must be delivered by the person solemnizing marriage to one of the parties joined in marriage.

FORM 1

# LAKE CARRIERS' ASSOCIATION

IDENTIFICATION CARD NOV 22 1934

*For Steamer* Crudoil

*Lying at* Shell Oil Dock River Rouge

*Recommended as* Watchman

LAKE CARRIERS' ASSOCIATION NOV 22 1934 ASSEMBLY ROOM, DETROIT

J W Westcott Jr

*Commissioner*

*Left office at* 11 40 Pm

Murdanie MacLeod

*Signature of Applicant*

*Discharge Book No.* 103179, *which is in his possession and must be presented with this card.*

THIS CARD WILL SERVE TO IDENTIFY THE APPLICANT FOR EMPLOYMENT IN GOING TO THE SHIP NAMED HEREON. THE LAKE CARRIERS' ASSOCIATION RECOMMENDS THE APPLICANT BUT DOES NOT ACT AS AGENT OF THE SHIP IN THE MAKING OF CONTRACTS OF EMPLOYMENT.

---

Form 979. (2d Ed.) (Ed. 11-30-29)

SERIAL NUMBER

190006

UNITED STATES
DEPARTMENT OF COMMERCE
STEAMBOAT INSPECTION SERVICE

File No. 8 6557

## CERTIFICATE OF SERVICE TO ABLE SEAMAN.

This is to certify that Murdanie MacLeod 27 years of age, born in Scotland, having given satisfactory evidence to the undersigned United States Local Inspectors, Steamboat Inspection Service, for the district of Buffalo, N.Y., that he has had the experience required by law, to all of which proof is made by affidavit, and having passed the examination as to eyesight, hearing, and physical condition prescribed by the Department of Commerce, is hereby rated as an Able Seaman for service on the High seas and any inland waters

Issued by the undersigned Board of Local Inspectors on this 7th day of July 1931

Signature of able seaman:

Murdanie MacLeod

James M. Ford
William P. Nolan

U. S. Local Inspectors.

# *BIBLIOGRAPHY*

### *Highland history*


*The Making of the Crofting Community*: James Hunter (John Donald)

*The Islands of Scotland*: Hugh MacDiarmid (Batsford)

*Old Statistical Account*

*New Statistical Account*

*Canna: The Story of a Hebridean Island*: J. L. Campbell (Oxford University Press)

*History of the Highland Clearances* (Vols I and I I): Eric Richards

*History of the Mathesons*: A. MacKenzie and A. MacBain (MacKay)

*Lewis: A History of the Island*: Donald MacDonald (Gordon Wright)

*The Hebrides*: W. H. Murray (Heinemann)

*Harris and Lewis*: Francis Thompson (David and Charles: Islands Series)

*The People's Clearance*: J. M. Bumstead (Edinburgh University Press)

*A History of Scotland*: J. D. Mackie (Pelican)

*The Highland Clearances*: A. Mackenzie (A. MacLaren)

*The Highland Clearances*: John Prebble (Secker and Warburg)

*History of the Outer Hebrides*: W. C. Mackenzie (A. Gardner)

*Public Administration in the Highlands and Islands*: J. P. Day (University of London Press)

*The Isle of Lewis and Harris*: Arthur Geddes

*The Highlands and Islands of Scotland*: W. C. Mackenzie (Moray Press)

*Crofting Years*: Frank Thompson (Luath Press)

*Skye and the Outer Hebrides*: W. Douglas Simpson (Robert Hale)

*Tong: The Story of a Lewis Village*: Tong History Society
*Surprise Island*: James Shaw Grant (James Thin)

### *Scottish/American history*

*The Scots Overseas*: Gordon Donaldson (Robert Hale)
*Colonists from Scotland: Emigration to North America (1707–83)* (Cornell University Press)
*Directory of Scottish Settlers in America (1625–1825)*: David Dobson (Genealogical Publishing)
*The Emigrant Scots*: Michael Brander (Constable)
*Highland Settler: The Scottish Gael in Nova Scotia*: Charles Dunn (University of Toronto)
*The Highland Scots in North Carolina*: Meyer (Chapel Hill)
*Scotus Americanus*: William R. Brock (Edinburgh University Press)
*Colonists from Scotland*: Graham (Kennikat Press)

### *Emigration (General)*

*Immigrant Groups in Canada*: ed. Elliot (Prentice Hall)
*British Immigrants in Industrial America*: Berthoff (Harvard University Press)
*Immigrants*: Harvey and Troper (Von Nostrand Reinhold)
*Emigration from the British Isles*: Carrothers (P. S. King and Son)
*The Search for Prosperity*: Richard Garret (Wayland)

### *Canada and USA*

*The Roar of the Twenties*: James H. Gray
*Detroit*: ed. Holli (Franklin Watts)
*Social Welfare in Ontario (1791–1893)*: Richard Splane (University of Toronto Press)
*Historical Statistics of Canada*: Urquhart and Buckley (Cambridge MacMillan)

*American Ethnic Groups*: Cordasco and Alloway (Scarecrow)
*Farmer Premier*: The Memoirs of E. C. Drury: (McLelland and Stewart)

### Leverhulme

*Viscount Leverhulme by his Son* (George Allen and Unwin)
*Lord Leverhulme*: W. P. Jolly
*Lord of the Isles*: Nigel Nicholson

### Opium War and Far East

*Foreign Mud*: Maurice Collis (Faber and Faber)
*The Opium War*: Brian Inglis (Coronet)
*British Trade With China* (Pamphlet): James Matheson (Smith Elder and Co.)
*The East India Company*: Brian Gardner (Hart Davis)

### Shipping

*Canadian Pacific Afloat* (CPR in Association with the World Ship Society)
*Merchant Fleets in Profile*: Duncan Haws (Patrick Stephens)
*Great Passenger Ships of the World*: Arnold Kludas (Patrick Stephens)

### Journals

*West Highland Mercenaries in Ireland*: Andrew McKerral (Scottish Historical Review Vol. XXX, 1951)
*James Matheson of the Lews*: A. MacKenzie (Celtic Magazine, 1882 and Private Pamphlet)

### Songs

*Eilean nan Fhraoich: Songs of Lewis* (Acair)

### *Parliamentary Papers*

*Overseas Settlement*: House of Commons Reports: 1919, 1920, 1921, 1922, 1923, 1924, 1925. Report of Committee: 1923. Empire Settlement Act: 1922.

*Landholders Acts*: 1886–1919

*Scottish Land Court Reports*: Vol. VIII (1919), Vol. XI (1923)

*Brand Report*: 1902

### *Others*

*Highland Journey*: Colin MacDonald

*I Crossed the Minch*: Louis MacNeice (Longman)

New York Telephone Directories

### *Newspapers consulted*

*West Highland Free Press*

*Stornoway Gazette*

*People's Journal*

*Glasgow Herald*

*The Scotsman*

*Edinburgh Courant*

*London Evening News*

*Toronto Star*

*Toronto Globe*

*Toronto Telegram*

*St John Daily Telegraph*

*The Bulletin*

*Eilean nan Fhraoich* magazine